MAKING PROJECT MANAGEMENT
WORK FOR YOU

Other titles in the Successful LIS Professional series

Sheila Pantry   Dealing with aggression and violence in your workplace
Tim Owen   Success at the enquiry desk
Beryl Morris   First steps in management

| THE SUCCESSFUL LIS PROFESSIONAL | SERIES EDITOR Sheila Pantry |

MAKING PROJECT MANAGEMENT WORK FOR YOU

Liz MacLachlan

LIBRARY ASSOCIATION PUBLISHING
LONDON

© Liz MacLachlan 1996

Published by
Library Association Publishing
7 Ridgmount Street
London WC1E 7AE

Except as otherwise permitted under the Copyright Designs and Patents Act 1988 this publication may only be reproduced, stored or transmitted in any form or by any means, with the prior permission of the publisher, or, in the case of reprographic reproduction, in accordance with the terms of a licence issued by The Copyright Licensing Agency. Enquiries concerning reproduction outside those terms should be sent to Library Association Publishing, 7 Ridgmount Street, London WC1E 7AE.

First published 1996

British Library Cataloguing in Publication Data
A catalogue record for this book is available from the British Library

ISBN 1-85604-203-0

Typeset in 11/14 pt Aldine 721 by Library Association Publishing.
Printed and made in Great Britain by Biddles Ltd, Guildford, Surrey.

Contents

Series Editor's preface   vii

Introduction   ix

Acknowledgements   x

1 **What is project management?**   1
   How to recognize a project   2
   The stages of project management   3
   Define   4
   Plan   5
   Implement, monitor, adjust   5
   Evaluate   6
   And finally   6

2 **Defining the project**   7
   Objectives   8
   Scope   9
   Constraints   11
   Getting approval   13

3 **Project organization**   18
   Project board – the main actors   18
   Reporting methods   22

4 **Planning the project**   25
   A good plan needs to be . . .   25
   A good plan outlines . . .   26
   Success factors   27
   The what – task analysis   28
   The when – scheduling   31
   The who – resource allocation   35
   And finally . . . deliverables   37

v

5 PM techniques   39
GANTT charts   39
Critical path method   41
PERT charts   42
Network analysis   43
Budget profiling   44
Risk analysis   47

6 Implementing the project   53
Doing the job   53
Monitoring   54
Dealing with change   57
Completion   58

7 What to do when things go wrong   60
How to spot problems   61
What to do when things go wrong   63
Exception reports   66
However . . .   67

8 Evaluation   68
Was it a success or a failure?   68
How do you measure success?   69
What could you have done better?   70
What have you learned about your environment?   72
And so on to the next one   73

9 The real world – multiple projects   74
Getting things done   74
Multiple projects   75
How project management software can help   76

Appendix 1   Further reading   79

Appendix 2   Project management software   82

Index   84

Series Editor's preface

With rapid technological advances and new freedoms, the workplace presents a dynamic and challenging environment. It is just these advances, however, that necessitate a workforce relying on its versatility and adaptability knowing that life-long full-time jobs are a thing of the past. Work is being contracted out, de-structured organizations are emerging and different skills and approaches are required from 'brain-workers' who must solve new and changing problems. All workers must become self-motivated, multi-skilled and constantly learning. Demonstrating the international economic importance of professional development, the European Commission has officially voiced its commitment to a European community committed to lifelong learning.

For the information professional, the key to success in this potentially destabilizing context is to develop the new skills the workplace demands. Above all, the LIS professional must actively prioritize a commitment to continuous professional development. The information industry is growing fast and the LIS profession is experiencing very rapid change. This series has been designed to help you manage change by prioritizing the growth of your own portfolio of professional skills. By reading these books you will have begun the process of seeing yourself as your own best resource and begun the rewarding challenge of staying ahead of the game.

The series is a very practical one, focusing on specific topics relevant to all types of library and information service. Recognizing that your time is precious, these books have been written so that they may be easily read and digested. They include instantly applicable ideas and techniques which you can put to the test in your own workplace, helping you to succeed in your job.

The authors have been selected because of their practical experience and enthusiasm for their chosen topic and we hope you will benefit from their advice and guidance. The points for reflection, checklists and summaries are designed to provide stepping stones for you to assess your understanding of the topic as you read.

Making project management work for you will give you, the information professional, a head start in learning how to identify a project, recognize the major stages of a project and get things done in time. It will also help you see when things are starting to go wrong and to take corrective action before it is too late.

Liz MacLachlan draws on her considerable experience as both a library and a project manager to provide real-life examples. Her step-by-step approach guides you through from the beginning to the end of your project. Having got there – was it a success? Liz gives advice on how to evaluate success, and how to learn from what went well and what went less well. Only then can you celebrate! May all your projects be successful!

Sheila Pantry

Introduction

Managing an information service in today's environment is an increasingly complex task. Electronic sources like the Internet offer new opportunities to develop the service – but these take time and thought and established services have to be maintained at the same time. More work, less time and never sufficient resources – how is the manager to decide between conflicting priorities?

Adopting a project management approach can help. Think of each task as a project – define your objectives, plan the timescale, allocate resources, monitor progress and evaluate what you have achieved. When you do this you will find you can see more clearly how tasks inter-relate, and will be able to plan realistically and understand how change in one area is likely to impact elsewhere. In this way you will be able to see how the new services can be fitted in, and how to get your team working together.

Project management is not just for the large, one-off projects such as building a new library or installing a computer system. It works for the individual information professional too. It can help you, whether you are managing a branch, section or just yourself, to sort out the important from the urgent, give you confidence to say yes (or no) to new work and to achieve more. In short to **manage** not just **cope** with your job.

Acknowledgements

I am grateful to the friends and colleagues who have helped with this book. In particular I would like to thank Ann Lawes and Nigel Oxbrow for sowing the seed, Alison Raisin, Julian Rowe, Anne Bridge, Richard Goodwin, Robin Goode and Michael Wild for the many discussions on how projects should be managed, and my husband for his support and advice.

I am also grateful to CCTA for permission to discuss the PRINCE project management methodology. PRINCE® is a registered trademark of CCTA. Although my experience has been gained in the public sector the views and mistakes are all my own.

Chapter 1
What is project management?

> In this chapter we take a look at what project management is. You will learn:
> ➤ how to identify a project
> ➤ what the major stages of a project are, and
> ➤ how they relate together.

The day after the Queen and President Mitterand opened the Channel Tunnel a cartoon appeared in the *Daily Telegraph*. It showed the Tunnel disappearing into the hillside, and beside it was a large sign:

> **Channel Tunnel
> twinned with the
> British Library**

This reflects a view that many people have of projects – that they are large-scale, high-profile disasters. Think of the Stock Exchange Taurus computer system, or the London Ambulance Service scheduler. But, despite the cases that hit the headlines, it is not a true picture. Many, many projects finish to time, on budget and do what was expected of them. Think also of the new Glyndebourne opera house, or the majority of motorway extensions. Why do some projects succeed while others fail? Basically, it is because they have been well managed.

Project management is about how to get things done. It is about deciding what you want to do, planning, doing the job, and monitoring progress so that you can see if things are starting to go wrong and correct them before it is too late. There is a lot of mystique about project management – difficult jargon and complicated diagrams. Large projects like the Channel Tunnel or the British Library **are** complex, and need teams of people to manage them. But smaller projects such as recataloguing a section of the library, or developing a new service for readers, also benefit from a project management approach. It is useful not just for one-off projects like construction works or new computer systems, but also for the regular small-scale tasks like current awareness bulletins or marketing activities – anything which you as a manager of a library or a section of a library, have to make happen. An understanding of the techniques of project management will help you to complete your projects more effectively, and to manage change instead of coping with it.

How to recognize a project

A project could be anything at all. Many winter mornings just getting out of bed and in to work can be a major project in itself. Most books on project management define a project as something which is new, but this is not entirely helpful. In today's busy world situations change so fast that a task completed successfully last year may be a quite different task this year. For our purposes a project is a task with a beginning, a middle and an end, which you as a manager need to complete. It will have:

- ➤ an objective – an outcome that you want to achieve;
- ➤ benefits – what you expect to achieve by the project;
- ➤ a timescale – when you want to achieve it by;
- ➤ costs – resources that you will need in order to achieve your objective and realize your benefits

Your project will not exist in isolation. There will be various factors surrounding it which will either help (opportunities) or hinder (constraints) or otherwise threaten the success of your project (risks). The purpose of project management is to try to identify all of these factors and plan for them so as to give you the best chance of success.

So, let's identify a couple of projects to see what they look like.

> ### Project 1 – Conducting a user survey
>
> A new librarian has just been appointed at Acme Foods. As part of an initial review of the services provided by the library the librarian wants to find out what the users think of them. A user survey seems appropriate. The **objective** of this project is to find out what users of the library think of the services it provides. The **benefits** expected are a ranking of importance of the different services to the users which will provide the basis of any changes. The **timescale** will depend on the deadline for the review and the **costs** will be mainly staff time in designing and running the survey.

> ### Project 2 – Installing the loans module of a computer system
>
> In this project let us assume that a small college library has been introducing an integrated computer system to manage the library gradually in separate modules. The catalogue is already in operation and the next module to be added is loans and reservations. The **objective** of the project is to computerize the loans and reservations function of the library. The **benefits** will come from a more rapid service for borrowers and better control of the stock. Because the work is disruptive to the normal work of the library the librarian has decided to install the system during the six-week summer vacation. The **timescale** is therefore fixed. The **costs** are the costs of buying and installing the system. This will include quite a number of incidentals such as bar-code labels, perhaps some new furniture and possible accommodation changes.
>
> The first project is small-scale and relatively simple. It will involve at most four people, and could as easily be done single-handed. Whereas the second project is quite complex. It will need a number of people to complete, and there are several risks and constraints around it which will need careful exploration. We will be coming back to both these projects throughout this book to look at what happens as they progress.

The stages of project management

Each project is made up of distinct stages. In the chapters which follow we will be going into all these stages in more detail.

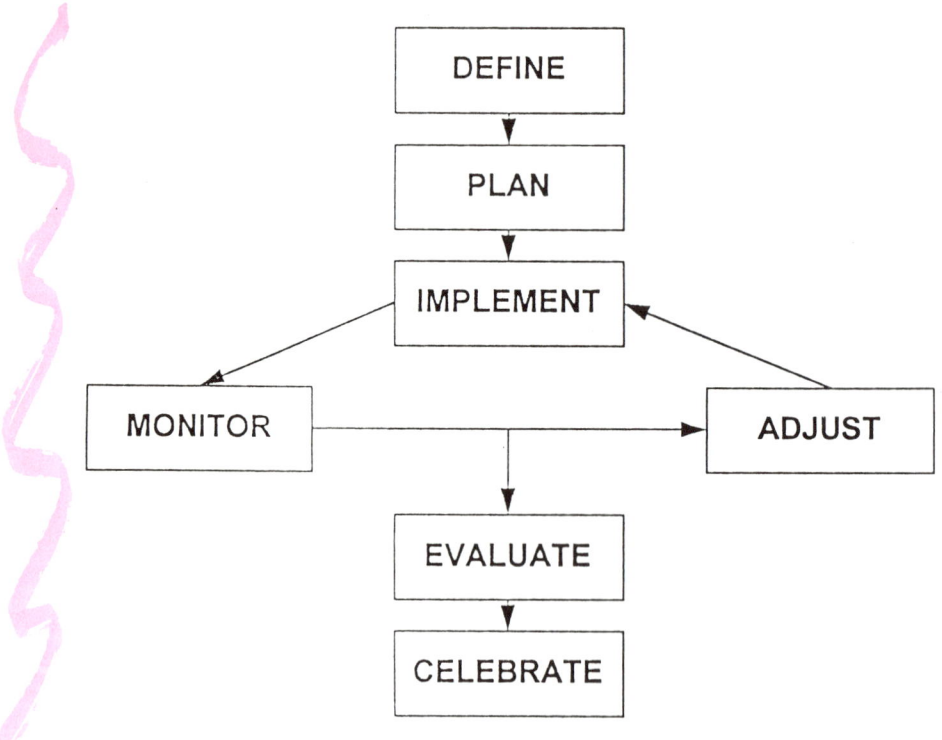

Fig. 1.1 *The stages of a project*

Define

The first stage is to **define** the project. What is it that you want to achieve? In this stage you think around the problem, possibly brainstorming with others. You decide the scope of the project, what will be included and, more importantly, what will not. This is the first danger point. Many projects go wrong at this stage because they do not define the scope of the project sufficiently clearly. In the User Survey project

What is project management?

example the librarian will need to decide whether the users should be asked about **all** the services, or only some of them. There will be different results, and a different outcome to the project, as a result of this decision. In the definition stage you will also think about the factors (risks, opportunities and constraints) which will affect the success of your project. You will do some initial planning – roughing out what tasks need to be done, and think about the resources needed. And you will think about the benefits you expect to flow from success. Depending on the size of your project, and the procedures in your organization, you may need to get **approval**, permission to start the project. This can be quite formal, requiring a **business case** to show that the benefits outweigh the costs before permission is granted. Or, for a small project it might just be a discussion with your boss.

Plan

Assuming that approval is given, the next stage is **planning** the project. This is the crucial stage of any project and where most of the textbooks tend to concentrate. We will look at some of the methodologies such as **critical path** and **risk analysis** in Chapter 5 Project management techniques. In the planning stage you sort out **who** does **what, when** and **in what order**. You decide the skills you need in the project team and identify other resources required, such as accommodation or equipment. You think harder about the constraints and risks of the project, and what you can do if things go wrong.

Having planned the project so thoroughly, all you now need to do is do it!

Implement, monitor, adjust

However, in the **implementation** stage you need to make sure that things go according to the plan. You need to **communicate** with everyone involved in the project, team members, your managers, other staff in the library, customers, perhaps the whole organization, to let them know how the project is going. You need to **monitor** progress, check that deadlines are being met, check that the quality of the work is what you expected, check that everyone understands what they are doing, check that the budget is on target. Always watch out for early signs of trouble so that you can **adjust** either the activities or the plan to put things back on course.

Evaluate

Strangely enough, many projects do not have a formal end – they just stop with everyone involved thankful it is over. Though understandable, this is a lost opportunity because it misses out the last two stages of the project. Whatever the outcome you should **evaluate** how it went. In every project there will be bits which went well, and other bits which went less well. Be honest! There is so much to be learned from examining not only what happened, but also why and how it could be avoided (or repeated) next time. A project gives team members the opportunity to show what they can do, possibly surprising both you and themselves. And a project also teaches you a great deal about the organization and environment you work in. Who was helpful and who was obstructive? What new facilities did you uncover, and what new connections were made? Whether the project has been fully, partially or not at all successful a thorough and open evaluation can give you valuable help for the future.

And finally

Don't forget to **celebrate**. Whatever happened, however successful or not, getting to the end of a project is an achievement. It should be marked – even if it's only with a thankyou to your team.

Chapter 2
Defining the project

In this chapter you will learn how to:
- ▶ define the objective
- ▶ scope the project
- ▶ identify constraints
- ▶ draw up an initial plan
- ▶ prepare a business case
- ▶ get approval.

'Would you please tell me, please, which way I ought to go from here?'
'That depends a good deal on where you want to go' said the Cat.

As in *Alice in Wonderland* so with projects. The very first step is to decide what it is you want to do. Are you planning to build an extension to the library, or install a computer system or define a new service or produce a reading list? When you get to the end of the project what will you have achieved?

Having a clear objective will help you to convince others that the project is worth while and to let you proceed in the first place. It will provide a vision for the others in your team and help them to see what their work is for. It will give you a point of reference during the project to monitor progress against, and will help you decide between different courses of action. And finally, it will let you know when you have finished, and you can start the celebrations! Knowing what you want to do will determine what will happen for the rest of the project. By beginning at the end with the desired result and working backwards the rest of the project will start to fall into place.

Conversely, lack of clarity at this stage will mean problems later on. So it is well worth while spending some time at the start deciding the objectives of your project. In fact, if you cannot articulate them clearly you should not start the project.

Objectives

Deciding on the objective is not easy. Project objectives do not form themselves. They are the result of discussions with other people who will be involved in the project.

In a service area such as a library this will begin with your **customers**. How will they be affected by the end result? In our User Survey example the benefit for the customer is direct – a service closely focused on their needs. In the Loans System example there is a direct benefit – less time queuing at the desk to have books issued – but there are also indirect benefits in the library staff having better control of the stock, better reservation procedures and time released from filing loans slips to spend with the customer. Don't forget to check whether your customers actually want what you are offering to them. And also be careful not to raise your customers' expectations by promising a change to them. There is a long way to go yet and this is just the start.

The next group to talk to are your **colleagues**. They will be the ones who will help you to turn a good idea into a project. What do they think about your idea? What is in it for them – in the Loans System less boring filing and more customer contact time. What will your project involve? How will it relate to their work, or to other projects they may have? What issues do they see in carrying forward the project – where are the opportunities, constraints and what are the risks for them? We are already beginning to put some shape into this project. You may need to discuss your project not just with your immediate work colleagues but also with other people inside and outside your organization, people who have relevant expertise to help with this initial, brainstorming stage.

Then, when you have your ideas in a rough order, you should talk to your own line **managers**. Be prepared to explain the benefits you see, and how your project fits in with your overall system objectives or business plan. Your managers should have a wider view not only of your objectives but also the organization's. So they should be able to tell you about developments which will help or hinder further progress. Perhaps the organization is about to standardize on PCs, and your project needs

Apple Macs. Or perhaps another project has fallen through and the budgetary authority is looking for a new project to spend the money. This is the first test of whether your project will go ahead or not. So think around your project and prepare your arguments.

- ➤ What do you want to do? Show them the vision.
- ➤ Why do you want to do it? What are the benefits and for whom?
- ➤ What is the likely cost and who will pay?
- ➤ How feasible is it? What do others think?

Having got your customers, colleagues and managers to agree that your idea is worth exploring you are ready to move on to the next stage – scoping the project.

Scope

Put very simply the scope defines what will be included in the project and what will not. This is important, and once defined you should **write it down.** In the course of the project there will be many occasions where you will be tempted to divert from your plan. Sometimes this will be to take advantage of an opportunity, sometimes because time or resources are tight and you want to take a short cut. Checking back with the project scope will help you to decide what to do.

To define the scope you need to refer back to your objective. What do you need to do to achieve it? Everything which contributes directly to the objective, that is everything which **must** do to achieve the goal, is within the scope of the project. Everything else is outside. This does not mean that you cannot include other tasks in the project, if there are the resources and time to do them. But it does mean that when push comes to shove it is the out-of-scope activities which are the ones that can be jettisoned.

Let's look at a couple of examples to make this clearer.

Project 2 – Installing the loans module

In this project the objective is quite clear – to computerize the loans and reservation functions. This will involve putting bar-codes in all loanable stock, and loading details of all authorized borrowers. Reference stock is not loanable so it is **outside** the scope, but maps can be loaned so they are **within** the scope. All the students, academic and administrative staff of the college are authorized borrowers. They are **within** the scope. But the staff and pupils of local schools are only allowed to use the library for reference so they are **outside** the scope.

The library will still want to have a record of the reference stock in the catalogue, and will want external users to register before they are admitted. However neither need to be included in the records to be added for the loans module.

Project 3 – Guidance material

In this project the objective is to provide staff electronically with a source of guidance material which is easy to maintain and always up-to-date. First problem is to define what is meant by 'guidance'. There is a very large amount of material which might be counted as guidance – manuals, notices, desk instructions, books, diagrams and databases. Each of these is different in form and layout. To tackle all of these at once would make a very complex project. The scope needs to be defined very clearly. For example, low-maintenance guidance that does not change much, such as terms of employment, could be left in hard copy but volatile information such as the telephone directory included. Guidance that only a few people see, such as security reports, might be kept on paper but material that everyone is interested in, such as pay scales, computerized.

This does not mean that other material will not be included later on. But with a project like this, which involves a radical change in the way that people work, it makes sense to start with a closely defined set of material and add in others when you are confident the project will work.

The project manager will use the project objectives to set criteria against which to decide what is:

➤ essential – the project must deliver these;
➤ desirable – these are included in the scope, but could be dropped without destroying the project;
➤ nice to have – if the project wins the lottery these are in!

But be careful. You can also draw the scope too tight. In Project 3 the project will need to do some work at the beginning to identify **all** the material which might be included and then choose the most important (in the sense of delivering the greatest benefit to the most people) to work on first. As the project proceeds the team must not forget the rest of the material. Otherwise the system may **only** deal with the subset and nothing else!

Constraints

No project exists in isolation. Some of your project will probably be defined for you because of legal or other requirements. These are called **constraints**. Despite the name, these are best thought of as defining the boundaries of your project rather than forcing you into a particular course of action. Identifying the constraints early in a project helps to set the scope, to make the task more manageable by ruling out some possibilities and so saves time and effort on blind alleys.

What must you do?

If you want to build a new library you will need planning permission. If you want to circulate a press cuttings bulletin you will need clearance from the copyright holders. If you want to install a computer system there will be health and safety regulations. In many projects there are **legal requirements** which must be complied with.

There may also be **standards** which apply to your project. A number of libraries have their services certified to BS EN ISO 9000 (formerly BS5750). If yours is one then any new service, or any change to an existing service, will need to satisfy the requirements of that standard. At the organizational level there may be a standard of developing databases in one particular software package. Or perhaps all documentation needs to conform to a stylesheet for consistent presentation of the company image.

Your organization may have established **working practices** which define the way that you can do things. There may be union agreements, for example, which determine whether or not you can employ someone on a short-term contract as part of the project team. Each of the major management consultancies has its own tested methodology for carrying out projects. In the public sector the PRINCE (PRojects IN Controlled Environment) methodology is widely used in IT projects.

You may also be constrained by what has gone before. In our Loans System example the librarian is constrained in the choice of software and cannot choose the 'best' on the market. The system must have **compatibility** with existing systems. If a similar project has not been successful you may be constrained by the negative **expectations** that the previous project has generated. Or if the previous project was very successful expectations may be over-positive. There is no easy way around this. Unrealistic expectations will cause problems unless they are identified, faced and managed by good communication throughout the project.

What assumptions are you making?

In project management terms **assumptions** are of two kinds, those we make consciously and those we make unconsciously.

We make the second kind of assumptions all the time, at work and at home. We assume that we can use the car on a particular evening, that our staff will remember when we are on leave, that we have told everyone on the team about the next stage, that everyone thinks the same way we do. Time and time again, like daleks faced with a flight of stairs, reality proves our assumptions wrong.

There is one sure way of dealing with this kind of assumption in project management. **Don't make any**. But more realistically, get into the habit of checking. Don't assume that a room or a piece of equipment will be available because you need it – check it out. Don't assume that members of your team are telepathic – have regular meetings with minutes and issue regular bulletins to keep them up to date. Don't assume that a job which experience has shown the accommodation section takes two weeks over can be done overnight – give them plenty of notice and add a safety margin.

But some things cannot be checked. You cannot know when you set your budget what the dollar exchange rate will be for journal subscriptions due in 12 months. You have to make the first kind of assumption, an educated guess, that it will be the same, or 10% higher or 10% lower. You cannot know that the library supplier will deliver all the books he or she has contracted to. You have to make an assumption, based on past performance, and trust that they will. However, whenever you make assumptions write them down. Any assumption is an area of uncertainty, and so in project management terms, a risk.

Risks

How to identify, analyse and measure risks is covered more fully in Chapter 5 Project Management Techniques, and what you can do about them is covered in Chapter 7 What to Do When Things Go Wrong. At this stage of defining the project all you need to do is to think about what could go wrong, and what the impact might be if it did.

Risks are about the project not going to plan. They are about resources or people not being available when you need them, about machines not working, about the outputs not being of the quality you were expecting. This can happen because of an unchecked assumption, or lack of realism in the planning, or poor organization or because you are trying to do something which is new and/or complex. If you are dependent on resources or factors outside your control the project is risky.

The impact of things not going to plan is in proportion to the importance of the project to your main business. If the Loans System falling behind means that you cannot access the catalogue you have a major problem. If it means that you have to continue with manual issue a little longer this is still a problem, but less critical.

Getting approval

The next step is to get formal approval to proceed. For this you will need an **initial plan** and some form of **business case** with an indication of costs and benefits. You will need to convince the approving authority both that the project is worth doing, and that you can be trusted to carry it out. The level of detail will depend on the nature of the project and your organization. Small-scale projects may be given the nod very informally after the first discussion with your boss. Each organization will have a procedure to be followed, which you should identify as part of your initial research and follow carefully. The remainder of this chapter deals with processes for the larger projects – but even very small projects can benefit from the same approach.

Initial plan

This first-stage plan will record all the research you have done so far. It will cover what you want to do and why and the constraints, assumptions and risks that you have identified.

It will outline the various **tasks** to be completed and put them into order. Chapter 4 Planning the Project sets out how to do this. At this stage you do not need to go into it in depth. But you need enough detail to show that the project is realistic. You should set out what tasks need to be done, and in what order. How long do you expect them to take and are any of them dependent on any other? You cannot issue a bulletin until you have selected the material to go into it. Issue is therefore dependent on selection.

Next comes **resources**. What skills do you need to carry out the project. Do the staff have these skills? If not, can this be remedied through training? Would it be better to employ an expert with the necessary skills for the time needed? Often this last option is not open to you, and you must make the best of what you have. But if the missing skill is critical to the success of the project it is worth arguing the case. Check also that the staff are available when you need them, and are not committed to another project.

What other resources do you need? If equipment has to be bought there will be a lead time before it can be delivered. If accommodation

Defining the project

changes are needed the same is true. In some organizations, where money is tight, even the supply of stationery has to be planned in.

What will be produced in the way of reports or other outputs? These are often called **deliverables** or **products** of the project. The authorizing body will feel more comfortable if it can see a list of outputs from each stage and so can check on the progress of the project.

Business case

In most projects you will need funds to carry it out. Even where no new money is needed there is still the opportunity cost – the cost of your not doing what you would have been doing if you had not been doing the project. So you need to produce a business case. The purpose of this is to estimate the costs and benefits of the project, and to convince the authorizing body that the project is worth the effort.

This can be a difficult exercise, especially for long-term projects. When Central London property prices were high a number of government departments relocated to towns such as Leeds, Newcastle and Liverpool to take advantage of cheaper accommodation. The business case looked good – the cost of relocation was quickly outweighed by the saving in rent. However the collapse of the property market in the late 1980s and the increase in travel costs changed the basic assumptions on which the policy was based. The **pay-back** – the period before the benefits overtake the costs – is now longer than originally anticipated.

Costs

Where are the main areas of cost? This is not only the cost of the resources used by the project, but may also include other costs incurred elsewhere. In Project 3 – Guidance material there will be a cost to the owners of the guidance of converting their information into a form suitable for the new system. Even in Project 1 – the User Survey there will be a cost to the users in the time spent filling in the questionnaire.

Benefits

Similarly, benefits may not all fall to the library. Project 2 – Loans System will free staff from having to operate a cumbersome manual issue

15

system, with all the filing, recalling and reminding. The library could choose to take the benefit in one of two ways. Either they will need less staff, or they can do more work with the same number. Either way they have a benefit. The benefit to the users will also be a time saving, and an improved level of service. The first can be quantified, the second is harder to demonstrate, but is still important.

Cost-benefit analysis

For large projects you may need to present the costs and benefits in the form of a **cost-benefit analysis** (CBA) or **investment appraisal**. Both have the same purpose, to show that the benefits outweigh the cost, that the pay-back period is acceptable and that the project is worth doing. There are many different ways of doing a CBA, most of which involve some mathematical adjustment to reflect the effects of inflation and the change in value of costs over time. Some include value added tax (VAT) and some don't. What matters is that you use the approved method for your organization.

Tolerance or contingency

Nothing in this world goes according to plan. Finally in your business case you should make allowance for the unforeseen and include an element for tolerance and/or contingency. These are usually expressed as a flat percentage. **Tolerance** is the amount of time you can slip in the plan without reporting back to the authorizing body and seeking permission to continue. **Contingency** is the amount you allow within your agreed budget for extra, unforeseen expenses. Tolerance and contingency are related to risk. The greater the risk, the more likely the project is to take longer and cost more – and the less likely the authorizing body is to give you a free rein! Tolerance of around 10% and contingency of 15% is usually about right for a medium-scale project taking no more than six months.

> **To sum up**
>
> **After you have:**
>
> ➤ agreed your objectives
> ➤ clarified the scope
> ➤ identified the major constraints and risks
> ➤ checked assumptions
> ➤ done your initial plan
> ➤ written a business case and
> ➤ got approval

you can consider your project well and truly defined. You are ready to move on to the next stage – **getting organized.**

Chapter 3
Project organization

> **In this chapter you will learn about:**
> - the main actors
> - the role of the project manager
> - reporting methods.

One of the main reason that projects fail is because they were poorly organized, often because nobody was responsible for their success. In this chapter we will be looking at the basic organization to get the project off to a sound start. Having got approval you will be very keen to get started right away. But taking a few days to get the basic responsibilities and ground rules sorted out will pay dividends later on.

Most of what follows is drawn from the PRINCE methodology, mentioned in the previous chapter. Although this was designed to manage IT project in the public sector the basic ideas and methods are just as useful in other projects and other sectors.

Project board – the main actors

We saw in Chapter 2 Defining the Project that there were a number of people concerned in the project. When deciding the objective you needed to talk to customers, colleagues, experts and managers. In presenting the business case you needed to get financial authority. There is a lot going on in any project and it is hard for one person to make sure that all the different interests are covered properly.

For this reason it is common practice to set up a project board to oversee the project and to help the project manager keep it on the rails. A typical project board structure is shown in Figure 3.1.

Project organization

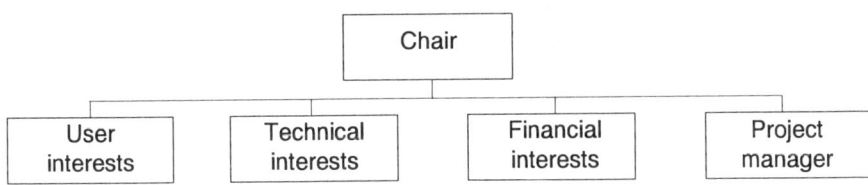

Fig. 3.1 *A typical project board structure for a small project*

The roles of these various actors are described below. The bigger and more expensive the project, the more formal the mechanisms will need to be. In smaller projects roles can be combined. The board should be big enough to represent all the major interests, but small enough to work – for medium-sized projects five to eight will be about right. But even in a single-handed project the project manager will find it useful to think separately about all the different interests.

It is sensible to identify the main roles for your project board as early as possible. Their experience will help when you are drawing up the initial plan and the business case, and will lend weight with the authorizing body when you get approval.

Chair

The role of the Chair is to take overall responsibility for the project, and to decide what to do if there is a conflict between different interests. Say the project was costing more than was in the budget. Finance might think the project should be stopped, but User might want to continue. It would be up to the Chair to take advice from other members of the board and decide what to do. Who should fill the role of the Chair depends on the project – the bigger the project the more senior the Chair. It should ideally be someone who has experience of projects in general. It must be someone who can see the big picture of what you are trying to do and who carries enough authority to support you when necessary.

User interests

Not surprisingly the user is representing the interests of the users of the eventual system. User interests can be very various. In large projects it is common to have several users, each representing a different community.

The Senior User (in PRINCE terms) is the person who has a business interest in the success of your project. He or she understands the project's objectives, can see the benefits to the organization and is responsible for seeing that the project delivers them.

But the Senior User can be just that – senior, and at some distance from the actual working process which will be affected by your project. If this is the case you may also need someone looking after the actual users' interests. The job of the User Assurance Coordinator (UAC) is to make sure that the users can use the system and that it will help them.

Technical interests

The role of the Senior Technical is to make sure that the system will work, is within the organization's overall strategy and will not conflict with other systems in use. Senior Technical is really an IT concept, though many library projects are now dependent on IT to deliver services.

The Senior Technical also has a sidekick – the Technical Assurance Coordinator (TAC), whose job it is to make sure that all the technical elements of the project are done properly. Even if your project is not an IT project you may still need someone looking after the technical interests. In a recataloguing project for example you would need someone with the right knowledge and experience to decide on the appropriate standard of cataloguing and classification, and then to ensure that the quality of the output met these standards.

Financial interests

Senior Finance is usually the person who takes responsibility for the business case, keeping an eye on the costs and benefits as the project progresses. This again is more necessary on large projects which may consist of stages each of which will need to be separately justified before proceeding. There may also be other financial aspects for the project to consider. All public-sector projects involving capital spend, i.e. money on things as opposed to people, must consider whether they can be financed by the private sector. The new Skye bridge is an example, where the Scottish Office ran a competition for a private company to build the bridge and to recover its costs through passenger tolls. It fol-

Project organization

lows that the Senior Finance needs to be familiar with the way that money is organized in the organization, and will very frequently come from its finance department.

In small projects the same person will also oversee the project's budget, making sure that the costs are as planned and paying bills. In larger projects this will be the job of the Business Assurance Coordinator (BAC), who will also act as secretary to the board – taking minutes, organizing meetings, progress chasing and generally supporting the project manager.

Project manager

The role of the project manager is to get the job done. This book assumes that *you* will be the project manager. You will draw up the plan. You will organize the teams to carry out the plan, coordinating activity so that things run smoothly. You will monitor progress against the plan and you will take corrective action when things go wrong. At the end you will be the one with the bouquets when the project is a success, and the brickbats if it isn't.

The project manager will work with the UAC, TAC and BAC on a daily basis. Together they form the PAT – the Project Assurance Team.

Let's look at one of our projects to see how all these roles fit together.

> ### Project 2 – Installing the loans module
>
> This project is quite important for the library's business and has a number of constraints, most notably on time, which will make it tricky to get right. The Chair should therefore be the deputy librarian. The head of readers' services could then be one Senior User, with perhaps a representative from the reader community as another. The system administrator of the OPAC would be Senior Technical. As the college is small there is no real need for UAC or TAC – these could be combined with the senior roles. The project manager could also take on BAC, or it could be delegated to a junior member of staff.

21

Reporting methods

Having got your board set up the other important area in getting organized is agreeing reporting methods. How are you going to communicate progress and issues on the project with

➤ the project board,
➤ your team,
➤ your users – or anyone else with an interest?

Reporting methods can be formal or informal, or a mixture of the two. But communication is one of the keys to success in project management and it does not happen by itself.

Reports to the board

You will usually use a formal report when reporting to the project board. Agree with them both what they want to know and how often you will report to them. They are likely to want to know the **highlights**:

➤ activities since the last report – what you have been doing, what has been completed and what started. You should also state here if a task has been delayed.
➤ planned activities – what is due to happen next according to the plan or, if there has been a problem, what needs to be done to resolve it.
➤ issues – what problems have arisen or are likely to arise. This is the area where the board are most likely to concentrate and where you as project manager can draw on their experience and influence. Perhaps a component has not been delivered – the technical interests could suggest another supplier. Perhaps staff have been off sick – the chair or the user interests could arrange for help from another section.
➤ budget – what has been spent and how much is left. Are you on target?

Reports should be short, preferably no more than a page of bullet points which focus the board's attention on the key issues. And they should be

Project organization

regular – in a three to six month project they should be about every two weeks. In a longer project you should still report to the board at least monthly.

Board meetings

Meetings take up valuable time, and your project board will all be busy people. Keep the formal meetings to a minimum, when you need to ask them to agree to something. This could be

- ➤ at the beginning of the project to approve the plan;
- ➤ at the end to agree that the project is finished.

but you are likely to need to meet at the end of each major stage to review the result and confirm what to do next.

Team meetings

You will be seeing your team all the time as the project progresses. Many issues can be raised and sorted out informally just through a quick discussion, before they ever become problems. However it is important that you as project manager sit down with the team and review progress formally once a week. What has been done, what's next, are there any problems, how are we doing against the plan? The outputs from these meetings are **checkpoint** reports. These cover the same subjects as the highlight reports, but should be more frequent (every week or fortnight). Their purpose is to help the team be clear about what they need to do.

Newsletters and other informal methods

Finally you may need to let other people know how the project is coming on. Users, other staff in the library, other staff in the organization will get to know that something is happening. If you don't tell them what it is they will make it up for themselves – and this could cause problems later on. Think how it feels to be stuck in a train in a tunnel. After a couple of minutes conversation dies, and people start to look anxious. But when the guard announces over the intercom that another train has broken down in front, and we will be moving in ten minutes people are reassured.

So, if your users are going to have disruption to their services because of your project let them know in good time what will happen when, so they can make other arrangements. Then if you need to close the library because the floors will be up you won't have quite so many aggrieved users with pressing deadlines. Catch and keep their interest with regular bits of news on progress – that way you have a potential pool of volunteers when you need any user feedback. Don't forget your colleagues elsewhere either. They may have to cover for you because of the project, or even to deal with the users who have not read your notice. Your colleagues will be more prepared to help out, and will do it better, if they know what is going on.

The method you use depends on what is available. Newsletters, posters and flyers are all cheap and easy to produce with a word processor and a photocopier. If you have an electronic bulletin board, or even a Web page, use that. What matters is that you get your message across effectively to the people who need to see it.

To sum up

To get organized you should:

➤ **make sure you have the business, user, technical and financial aspects of the project covered;**
➤ **sort out how and when you will communicate with your board, team, users and other interested parties.**

Now it's time to settle down to some serious planning.

Chapter 4
Planning the project

> In this chapter we are looking at planning. You will learn:
>
> ➤ what makes a good plan
> ➤ about success factors, what they are and how to use them
> ➤ how to decide what needs to be done
> ➤ about planning when it is done . . .
> ➤ . . . and who does it
> ➤ how to identify the other resources you might need
> ➤ and about what is produced at the end of the project.

I once had a boss who had written above his desk

> Failing to plan
> is
> Planning to fail

That may be putting it a bit strongly, but only a bit. At the heart of every successful project lies a good plan. Whatever you are trying to achieve, from building a new library to organizing the Christmas party a good plan will get you from beginning to end with the minimum of fuss and the best chance of success. So what makes a good plan?

A good plan needs to be . . .

➤ **specific**. The plan should set out clearly what has to be done. Clear instructions are easier to follow. For the Christmas party the plan would go something like – decide date, book the room, organize helpers, send out invitations, collect money, buy food and drink, accept thanks! Sort out the Christmas party is just not specific enough.

- **measurable**. If you can measure a task you know what you have done and what more there is to do. In a recataloguing project count the books at the beginning. Then you have a measure of whether you are 10%, 60% or 95% finished.
- **accepted**. You are dependent on other people to carry out your plan. If they are uncertain about what they should be doing, or do not agree with it, they will not perform well. Much better to spend a short time at the beginning discussing the plan, taking their ideas on board and getting agreement than a long time towards the end of the project, when time may be short, going back to first principles.
- **achievable**. Optimism is a wonderful thing, and without some optimism we would never start anything at all. But do not expect everything to work out perfectly. If you need 15 man days to complete a task, but only have 10 – think again. It may not be worth starting a project if you know you cannot finish it.
- **timely**. Deadlines are not just there to be missed. They help to maintain momentum in a project, as well as measuring progress. They let everyone know when things should be done by and so encourage people to do what they need to so that the project can progress.

A good plan outlines . . .

- **what** is to be done. It will set out the tasks making up the project, and put them into a logical order. If there are a lot of tasks they may be grouped into stages. The plan will identify which tasks are dependent on other tasks, which are critical to the success of the project and which are not.
- **when** it needs to be done. When we were Defining the Project in Chapter 2 we started at the end with what we wanted to achieve. So too in planning. Start at the end – when do you need to have completed the project by, and work backwards. This usually shows that you should have started three months ago! But do not be downhearted, try again adjusting the scope of the project if necessary to get a realistic timescale.

➤ **who** does what. Make it quite clear who is responsible for which tasks, and let everybody else know. That way people will work as a team, they will trust one another and – very important – they will need less input from the hard-pressed project manager.
➤ **how** you will know when you have succeeded. As we saw in Chapter 1 many projects do not end, they simply stop. Setting out your success factors in the plan means that you have a stake in the ground of what you intended to do against which you can measure both progress and achievement.

Before we go on to look in detail at the what, when and who of planning, let's just take a minute to look at the how – success factors.

Success factors

Success factors (also know in jargon as critical success factors or CSFs) are all too do with the **quality** of the project and may be pulled together into a separate **quality plan**. They are based on the objective for the project, but take a step further on. At the high level they set out the **outcomes** that must be present at the end for the project to be considered a success. At the working level they set out the **standards** which must be met to reach those outcomes. In some types of project, particularly construction-type projects, the quality plan is very detailed and becomes in fact a specification. In management projects it is rarely possible to be so precise, but having an idea of what is acceptable and what is not is useful throughout the project. Let's look at some examples.

The objective of our User Survey is to find out what users think of the service the library provides. To do this the librarian will need enough users to respond to the questionnaire to give confidence that the view expressed are generally held. The librarian's first decision will be the number of users to send questionnaires to, and the number of completed forms returned which will provide a secure base for decisions. Response rates for mailed questionnaires are usually quite low. So, in Project 1 one success factor might be getting more than 40% of questionnaires returned. If only 35% are in by the time that analysis needs to begin the project manager will need to consider whether to chase non-respondents again, delay the analysis, or accept a lower standard. Another success fac-

27

tor would be getting enough information to form a clear view of user requirements – in other words having a good design. If the pilot showed that respondents were misinterpreting the questionnaire some redesign would be necessary.

In each project there is likely to be a range of success factors – some **essential** and some merely **desirable**. In Project 2 (the Loans System) essential success factors would be having the library open for business on the first day of the new term with all the borrower records loaded and the reservation function working. Having all the stock bar-coded and ready for loan is highly desirable, but the project might still be successful if only the short loan collection was ready. The other stock could be bar-coded on issue.

From these examples we can see that success factors not only provide a measure for evaluation at the end but they also help with planning the project. They identify the **critical** tasks – those that must be done for the project to be completed. In the User Survey looking at the success factors identify the questionnaire design and response rate as critical to achieving the objective. Therefore in the planning the librarian must make sure enough effort is put into these. In the Loans System the building works and conversion of personnel records are critical tasks. In a project with a restricted timescale preparatory work such as agreeing the building design and perhaps moving some non-essential stock could be done in advance, so that work could begin on day 1.

So now let us look in more detail at planning the tasks.

The what – task analysis

In time management there is a technique called eating the elephant. At the start a job to be done can look like a huge elephant sitting on your plate. You think you will never be able to eat it. That's true, you can't eat it all in one go. But if you chop the elephant up into bits you can eat a leg here or a trunk there, and before too long all that is left is bones and you have done it!

So too in project management – chop the project up into chunks (or tasks) and you can then put them into a logical order to reach your goal. It's much easier to see this in an example.

Project 1 – User Survey

The first thing to be done is to **decide on the purpose of the survey**. This will determine what you ask in the questionnaire and how you analyse the results. If you want ideas for new services you will give respondents plenty of space to write their own thoughts. If you want them to choose between services you will need to get them to indicate relative importance, perhaps by ranking.

Next **decide on the analysis method**. This may seem strange, but how you are going to analyse the data will determine the sort of questions you ask. If you want to be able to make statements of the kind '70% of users thought the library was very good or excellent' you will want a database or spreadsheet to do the number crunching – set up to match the tick boxes on your questionnaire. This speeds up the transfer of the data, and you can even get other people to help you. If you start with the questionnaire (the apparently logical way) you may be left with an awful lot of forms to read, and not be able to demonstrate clear conclusions at the end.

Now you can **design the questionnaire**. There are many books about questionnaire design – but the golden rule is to be clear about the purpose of each question. If you don't know what you are going to do with the response that you get, don't ask the question.

Next, **select recipients**. What characteristics should they have? Do you want to include only users, or non-users of the service as well? Do you want to survey everyone, or just a percentage? What is the realistic number of responses you need for a valid result ? (look at your success factors). That, multiplied by your expected response rate will give you the minimum number of questionnaires you will need to send out – add a few more for safety.

Having done all that, **send out the questionnaires** and **wait for replies** to come in. After a while you will need to **chase non-respondents** until you reach your target number. **Analyse the results**, then **write the report** and **present conclusions** perhaps to your team or senior management.

Dependent, parallel and overlapping tasks

If we now look more closely at the ten tasks making up our User Survey project we can see that we cannot do some of them until others are complete. So we cannot *send out the questionnaire* before we have *designed it* or before we have *selected the recipients*. Sending out the questionnaire is therefore **dependent** on the previous two tasks.

But *designing the questionnaire* and *identifying the recipients* are not dependent on each other. They could be done at the same time. They are **parallel** tasks. In the same way waiting for replies and *chasing non-respondents* are parallel tasks. It makes good sense with any questionnaire or survey to set an early deadline and to chase up late replies promptly.

You could also start to analyse some of the results before you have them all in. *Chase non-respondents* and *analyse results* are **overlapping** tasks. But you cannot present the report before you have written it. Presentation is dependent on writing.

Staging

Project 1 is a simple project with a short duration. Even so it falls into distinct **stages**. Stage 1 is the design stage – *deciding on the purpose, designing the analysis method* and *questionnaire* and *identifying the respondents*. Stage 2 is the research stage – *sending out the questionnaire, waiting for replies* and *chasing*. Stage 3 is analysis and presentation – analysing the results, *writing* then *presenting the report*. Stages are related tasks which group naturally together. Not all tasks from one stage need to be finished before you move on to the next – overlapping tasks like *chasing* and beginning the *analysis* can overlap stages as well – but an earlier stage must be completed before a later stage can end.

Stages are essential to organize and control the more complex projects. A very large project such as the Channel Tunnel will be planned in many stages – each of them projects on their own – and all having to be scheduled in so that necessary steps are complete in time for the next. There is no point in the track project being ready if the mining engineers are only half way across! Which brings us on to . . .

PLANNING THE PROJECT

Milestones

Within each project you need to build in points where you can pause to see where you are and to measure progress against the plan. In the User Survey suitable points might be sending out the questionnaire, deciding that enough responses had been received to stop chasing and making the final presentation. These are **milestones** – significant events or decision points in your project. If your project is organized into stages then it is usual to have a milestone at the end of each stage – often a project board meeting where the outcome of that stage is reviewed.

Milestones keep the project moving, and reaching them is a good sign that the project is on track. If you are driving from London to Glasgow you might expect to pass (on the West Coast motorway) close by Birmingham, Preston and Carlisle. Each of these milestones would tell you how your journey was proceeding. If you suddenly saw a sign saying 'York 2 miles' you would know you had taken a wrong turning!

In looking at milestones we have already begun to look at the next element of the plan.

The when – scheduling

Having identified the tasks you now need to think about how long each of them might take. Some tasks are **unit** based, e.g. there is a known number of books to be catalogued, or reminders to be sent out. The time taken for each unit can be measured and multiplied up to give the **duration** of the task.

Be realistic. Say that a working day is eight hours and it takes 15 minutes on average to catalogue a book. It does not follow that one person can catalogue 32 books in a day! That would allow no time to take their coats off, talk to colleagues about the awful journey they have had, make a cup of coffee (and other essentials) or to think about what they are doing, answer queries from the enquiry desk or discuss a classification number with their boss. In calculating how long tasks take most planners assume between 60% and 70% efficiency – so it is more reasonable to expect our cataloguer to get through around 20 books in an average day. In calculating longer periods remember to allow for holiday, training and illness in your estimates.

Other tasks are **activity**-based, i.e. the task is a single unit, and it takes as long as it takes. Experience will tell you how long it takes to design a questionnaire, or to write a report. Use this in planning to give yourself an estimate of the duration of the task.

Sometimes it is very difficult to estimate duration accurately. One way of coping with this is to use the **PERT** method of estimating (PERT will be explained in Chapter 5). To do this work out for each task:

O the most optimistic estimate of time
L the most likely estimate
P the most pessimistic estimate

The duration will be (O + [4 × L] + P) / 6. So if you think it will probably take 15 days to analyse the replies of the questionnaire, but if you work hard it might only take 8, but, on the other hand, if something else crops up it might take 20 – then the duration is (8 + [4 × 15] +20) / 6, or 14.6 days.

In our example most of the tasks are activity-based, though analysing the replies could be in part unit-based – the time taken to enter a single reply onto a spreadsheet.

Table 4.1 gives a rough indication of how long each of our ten tasks might take.

Table 4.1 Duration of tasks in Project 1

Task		Duration
1	Decide on purpose of survey	1 day
2	Design analysis method	2 days
3	Design the questionnaire	2 days
4	Select recipients	5 days
5	Send out the questionnaires	1 day
6	Wait for replies	25 days
7	Chase non-respondents	10 days
8	Analyse the results	15 days
9	Write the report	5 days
10	Present conclusions	1 day

Planning the project

Elapsed time, slack and lag

While duration is a useful measure of how long an individual task might take it does not tell us how long the overall project will be. Adding all the figures together gives a total of 67 days. But we have already seen that some of the tasks are parallel. By selecting the recipients at the same time as tasks 2 and 3 we can save four days. By setting a deadline of ten working days for replies and beginning to chase non-respondents after 11 days we can save ten days. By beginning to analyse the results 20 days after the questionnaires went out we can save another five days. If all of this works we could complete the project in 48 days!

The total time from beginning to end is called **elapsed time**. The nature of the tasks – whether they are dependent, parallel or overlapping – will affect the elapsed time of the project. So too will the amount of resources which can be deployed. Being able to run the design and selection tasks in parallel assumes that there are different people doing the two tasks. If not, if there is only you, then the tasks go back to being dependent.

However, this timescale is very fast. It might be as well to build a little time back in for reflection. Perhaps you would like to try the questionnaire on a few volunteers to see if it works before you send it out – add five days. Perhaps you would like to think about the draft report or circulate it to your colleagues before you present it to the board – add five days for that. Our project will now take 58 days.

Delay deliberately built into a project is called **slack**. It is always sensible to build some slack into a timetable. As well as providing useful reflection time it is also there in case some tasks over-run, as most assuredly they will. It is also useful to build more slack in towards the end of the project rather than the beginning to keep momentum going.

A different sort of delay is **lag** (also known as **lead time**) which occurs between dependent tasks. If you are decorating a room you need to let the paint dry before you hang the paper. Overlapping tasks have an in-built lag – you need to allow time for some of the questionnaires to be returned before you can start to analyse the results. In this example there is a lag between the start of task 6 and the start of task 8 of 20 days.

Making project management work for you

Lag is often the result of a constraint, such as a legal requirement. Any project in the public sector which involves purchasing goods or services above a financial limit needs to invite bids from all companies in the European Communities by advertising in the *Official journal*. This builds in a minimum three-month lag to the project.

Windows of opportunity

Where you have lag you also have windows of opportunity. These are dead times when you are waiting for something else to happen, and when you might be able to bring a task forward and so save time later on. Waiting for the responses to the questionnaire is just such a dead time. Bringing forward the start of the analysis fills part of this window of opportunity. Deciding on a report format and going on a presentation skills course are other possible fillers!

Windows of opportunity are very valuable to any project, and always watch out for them. Projects have an innate tendency to slippage, and bringing tasks forward whenever possible helps to counteract the drift.

Scheduling

The final 'when' task is scheduling. Having identified all the tasks, their duration and their relationships to each other you now need to give each of them start and finish dates. In the next chapter Project Management Techniques we will look at how to draw GANTT charts to schedule a project. But you don't need complex software to do it. Most projects are constrained by time – that is, they have to be completed by a certain date, because that is when the financial year ends, or the Queen comes to open the extension. If your project is like this, start at the end, with the completion date for the project and work backwards, slotting in each of the tasks with its dependencies and each of the milestones in turn.

So, if we want the presentation to go to the board on 30 September (the day before the Chief Executive goes on holiday) and our project takes 58 working days elapsed time we need to start on 16 July.

This will also show up the **deadlines**. If milestones mark the progress of the project, deadlines show how fast (or slow) we are getting there. On the journey to Glasgow, leaving London at 06.30 and travelling at a steady 60 miles an hour you would expect to get to Birmingham round about 08.00, and Glasgow (allowing for breaks) by 16.00. If you reached Birmingham by 10.00 you would expect to be late to your destination. End dates are obvious deadlines in a project, though tasks of long duration will have various checkpoints within them.

It is not at all uncommon to find that the dates do not work out and you cannot complete the project within the available time. If this is the case look at the end date – is it essential that you hit it? It is not worth endangering the project to meet an artificial deadline. If the end date is immovable you will need to modify the plan – either by adding in additional resources so that you can accomplish more in the same time or by changing the scope (attempting to do less with the resources you have). More detail on how to do this can be found in Chapter 7 What To Do When Things Go Wrong.

The who – resource allocation

The final part of planning is working out the resources – the people, equipment and materials – you need. Resources cost money and you have a set budget which the project board have approved. So you also need to work out what these resources will cost and whether you can afford them. We'll look at how to do this (budget profiling) in Chapter 5 Project Management Techniques.

Most important first.

People

In the initial plan in Chapter 2 we looked at the skills necessary for the project. Staying with the User Survey you might need questionnaire design and database construction skills in the design stage. Later on you might need analytical skills to draw conclusions from the replies, written communication skills to write the report and oral communication skills to present it convincingly. You need Superman (or Wonderwoman) – or more realistically you need to identify and develop these skills in the people working with you.

Once you know what skills you need, and who has them you are ready to give responsibility to individuals for particular tasks. Perhaps Jane has good analytical skills, so she would design the analysis method, help with the questionnaire and analyse the results. Perhaps Mary has experience in questionnaire design – she would take the lead on that, with Jane advising. Selecting the interviewees is likely to be a big task and you need knowledge of the organization. Have Jane and Mary and Fred and Bill on that. You will end up with a task allocation table which looks something like Table 4.2.

Table 4.2 Task allocation table

Task		Duration	Names
1	Decide on purpose of survey	1 day	Fred
2	Design analysis method	2 days	Fred, Jane
3	Design the questionnaire	2 days	Jane, Mary
4	Select recipients	5 days	Fred, Mary, Jane, Bill
5	Test questionnaire	5 days	Mary
6	Send out the questionnaires	1 day	Bill
7	Wait for replies	25 days	
8	Chase non-respondents	10 days	Bill
9	Analyse the results	15 days	Jane
10	Write the report	5 days	Fred
11	Present conclusions	1 day	Fred

Availability

Now you need to add in the start and finish dates of your tasks, and check whether the people you want are available on those days. Availability does not just mean they are not on holiday. It also means that they can spare time from their other commitments to work on your project. So the earlier you can let people know how much time you will need from them when, the better. If the people you want cannot be available when you want them you will either have to adjust your plan or reassign the task.

PLANNING THE PROJECT

Other resources

At this stage you should also schedule in the other resources you will need to do your project. These could be equipment, accommodation and materials that will be used during the project. In the User Survey you will need to print your questionnaire and send it out – what is the lead time for the **printers** or **reprographics** to produce the finished product? You will need to book a room and an overhead projector or other equipment for the final presentation. You will also need to book time in the board's diary so you have an audience! Think about what you need, when you need it, how long it takes to get it and organize it in good time.

Other resources are often less easy to re-organize than people. If accommodation is being built for your project you may not be able to speed it up to take advantage of a window of opportunity. Usually you are dependent on others, outside the project to deliver the equipment etc. that you need. Your priority is one among many and delays can occur. Make sure that all orders and instructions are in writing, that your suppliers know your timescales, get a written delivery or completion date and check on progress.

People can also be an other resource if you are buying in expertise from outside your immediate line management control. Here too flexibility is likely to be limited and you may need to work around when the expert is available.

And finally . . . deliverables

With tasks identified and scheduled and resources allocated the plan is very nearly complete. The final thing to do is to set out what you expect to deliver in the way of **deliverables** (also known as **products**) from the project. The main result will of course be the objective of your project – a better understanding of user needs, a new loans system. But on the way you will be producing other things – mostly documents, but also possibly verbal reports, seminars etc. In the User Survey there will be the plan, the questionnaire, the report and the final presentation. These are tangible outputs from the project. They give a measure of the quality of the project, in terms of its accuracy and completeness. They could also serve as milestones, and might be marked on the plan. When the deliv-

Making project management work for you

erable is complete, approved and on time you are on the way to Glasgow not Penzance!

In some project management methodologies (most notable PRINCE) a list of deliverables is included in the plan. This might set out:

➤ what the deliverable is – questionnaire, report etc.;
➤ who is responsible for producing it;
➤ when it will be produced;
➤ what sources will be used to produce it;
➤ what criteria or standards will be used to assess its quality and who will review it.

While product or deliverable lists are most applicable for large projects they can be useful also in smaller projects to set out clearly what is expected.

To sum up

Planning involves setting out:

➤ what tasks need to be done
➤ which are dependent on others
➤ how long they will take
➤ in what order they should be done
➤ who will do them
➤ what other resources will be needed
➤ what deliverables will be produced.

The next stage is implementing the project. But before we do, let's just take a look at some of the techniques you might use, or jargon you might encounter in project management.

Chapter 5
PM techniques

> In this chapter we look at some of the formal techniques used in project management and explain some of the jargon. It will cover
>
> ➤ GANTT charts
> ➤ PERT charts
> ➤ critical path method and network analysis
> ➤ risk analysis
> ➤ budget profiling.

So far we have been planning the project in a very common-sense way. But of course what seems obvious and simple now is based on the hard-won experience of many earlier project managers, particularly those working in the defence industries of the UK and USA. Much of the theory of project management was developed in the 1950s in response to the increasing complexity of the end results sought, and the growing need to achieve those end results more quickly and more cheaply than the competition.

The theory of project management seems full of jargon, but in essence all it is doing is expressing the same ideas as we have been looking at so far. In this chapter we will try to explain what the terms mean, and what the various diagrams and charts are used for in project management.

Let's begin with the most popular of all project management graphics – the GANTT chart.

GANTT charts

The first question about a GANTT chart is usually 'what do the letters stand for'. In this case it is not a what but a who – Henry L. Gantt, an American industrial engineer who invented them in 1917, during the First World War. Mr Gantt's basic idea was very simple. He took a stan-

MAKING PROJECT MANAGEMENT WORK FOR YOU

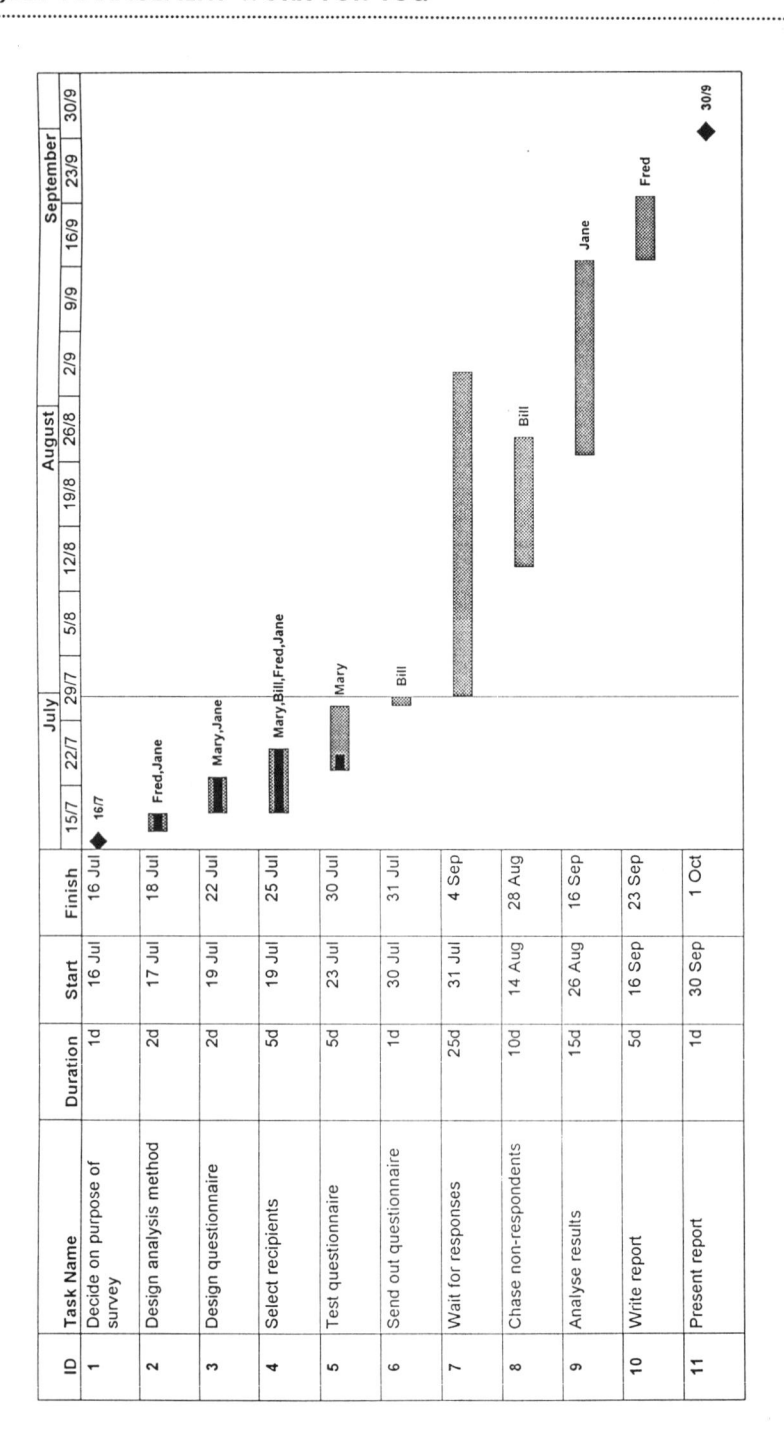

ID	Task Name	Duration	Start	Finish
1	Decide on purpose of survey	1d	16 Jul	16 Jul
2	Design analysis method	2d	17 Jul	18 Jul
3	Design questionnaire	2d	19 Jul	22 Jul
4	Select recipients	5d	19 Jul	25 Jul
5	Test questionnaire	5d	23 Jul	30 Jul
6	Send out questionnaire	1d	30 Jul	31 Jul
7	Wait for responses	25d	31 Jul	4 Sep
8	Chase non-respondents	10d	14 Aug	28 Aug
9	Analyse results	15d	26 Aug	16 Sep
10	Write report	5d	16 Sep	23 Sep
11	Present report	1d	30 Sep	1 Oct

Fig. 5.1 *A GANTT chart for the User Survey project*

dard bar chart and turned it on its side so plotting tasks onto a timescale showing start and finish dates. Figure 5.1 shows the GANTT chart for the project we planned in Chapter 4 – the User Survey.

Looking at this chart we can see at a glance the overall timescale of the project and the varying durations of each task. We can also see something of the task relationships. *Designing the questionnaire* and *selecting the recipients* are parallel tasks so they have the same start date. *Waiting for replies* is a long task, and we have quite a lot of flexibility before we need to begin *chasing non-respondents*. And the delay for reflection between *writing* and *presenting the report* shows up clearly. Milestones – our decision points – show up as diamonds.

The chart also shows what should be happening when. If we drop a vertical line for the current date and mark how far we have got with each task with a thin black line we can also use the GANTT chart to monitor progress. So here we can see that *testing the questionnaire*, which should have been finished, is only 25% complete. We will need to replan the rest of the project dates to see how this will impact on the project as a whole. If a task were to finish early the GANTT chart would also help to see whether other tasks can be brought forward.

GANTT charts are widely used because they give an immediate impression of the project. The example was created using project management software, but – as a GANTT chart is only a bar chart on its side – you can draw them with spreadsheets, word processors or even freehand. The bars themselves can be blocks, lines, crosses or anything else that takes your fancy. Several office equipment suppliers make bar chart kits to hang on the wall, complete with plastic or magnetic strips. GANTT charts are very good at giving an overall impression of the timescale of a project, and are particularly useful for simple projects of the kind we have been looking at. For most of the projects I have dealt with in libraries they are the main planning and monitoring tool. But if your project is complex or you need to keep track of multiple dependencies, you may need something more sophisticated.

Critical path method

We have already used the word 'critical' in looking at planning for tasks which must be done to ensure the project's success. The critical path method (CPM) is about time, and the critical path is the sequence of tasks which add up to the longest total time needed to complete the project. Like most project management methodologies CPM is an American invention – devised by Du Pont and Remington Rand in the 1950s to improve project scheduling techniques.

The way it works is to look at all the tasks, with their durations and dependencies. It then calculates two dates for each task on the entire schedule – the earliest start date and the latest possible end date. Those tasks where the dates are the same are **critical**, those where there is a difference (that is where you can identify slack) are **non-critical**. Any delay to a task on the critical path will delay the project. Non-critical tasks have slack time built into them, so that they can be delayed up to that point without endangering the project's deadline. Where you have parallel tasks the one that takes the shorter time will usually be non-critical.

However things do not stand still. As the project progresses your plan will turn into action, and the planned dates will become real. If you find that a critical task takes less time than you planned it may move **off** the critical path. If delays occur in a non-critical task and all the slack time is used up, then it will move **onto** the critical path.

Again, it is easier to understand this from a diagram, and the PERT chart is the graphical representation of CPM.

PERT charts

PERT is an acronym, it stands for Project Evaluation and Review Technique. PERT charts show the relationships of the tasks in a project and the order in which they need to be done. Just as the GANTT chart is a variation on a **bar** chart so a PERT chart is basically a **flow** chart.

PERT charts are more complicated than GANTT charts, and because they are usually not drawn to scale they do not show as easily where you are at any one time in the project. They consist of three elements as shown in Figure 5.2.

PM TECHNIQUES

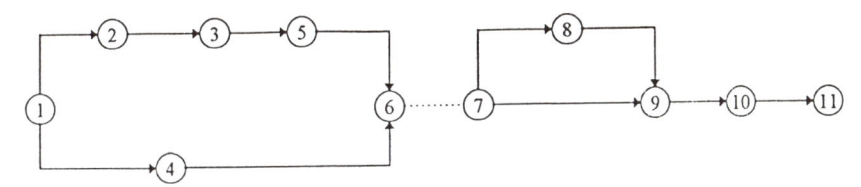

Fig. 5.2 *A PERT chart for the User Survey project*

- **events**, represented by circles, in our example events are things like 'questionnaire completed' or 'enough responses received';
- **activities** (what we have up to now called tasks, the things you need to do to achieve the events) are shown by arrows;
- **non-activities** (dependencies for which no work is required) are shown by dotted lines.

The advantage of the PERT chart is that the sequence of each activity is very clearly displayed, and the dependencies are obvious. Where your project is complex, with many parallel tasks done by different people, coordination becomes quite difficult. It is for these types of project that PERT charts are most useful. They really come into their own with large construction or manufacturing projects, and will usually be broken down into stages with separate charts for each stage. Each team will have their own charts, showing the activities they are responsible for, with the points where their work intersects with others showing up as milestones. If your project involves building, or a major IT installation, then it is likely that PERT charts will be used.

Network analysis

PERT charts and CPM both belong to a whole family of planning and control techniques called network analysis. Other terms you might come across are Critical Path Scheduling (CPS) and Critical Path Analysis (CPA) and there are several others. They are all based on the idea of the 'network' or 'arrow' diagram. The example in Figure 5.2 is the simplest form of PERT chart. Some types of charts show the duration of each activity by writing it in along the line. The most sophisticated versions, usually generated by computer programs, will draw the charts against a horizontal timescale with the length of line indicating how long an activity is expected to take, and any additional slack made up by a dotted line. Some of the books in Appendix A, particulartly Dennis Lock's *Project management*, cover all the techniques of network analysis in more detail.

However all these techniques are really just formalizing the processes we looked at in Chapter 4 on Planning the Project. They all deal with **what** needs to be done **when** and by **whom**. These questions lead on to **how much**, and the technique which covers that is budget profiling.

Budget profiling

Getting the budget right makes all the difference between success and failure in a project. Briefly, to profile the budget you need to take the project plan, and the resources allocated and work out

➤ how much these will cost and
➤ in which period (usually months) you expect to spend them.

The initial profile is important because, as we will see in the next two chapters, project spend is one of the main ways that you will monitor the project. And one of the first indications when things are not going according to plan.

How much

Broadly the costs of a project are one of three types:

➤ people, both your own staff and others, e.g. consultants, whom you buy in for a particular task;
➤ equipment (including computer hardware and software);
➤ expenses.

People costs are usually the largest element in library projects. Some organizations do not cost their own staff against a project, arguing that their salary would need to be paid anyway. But others do, and you need to check what applies in your case. Working out the cost is, in theory, simple. Take the annual cost of each person, divide by the number of working days to get the day rate, then multiply by the number of project days. But the calculations can be tricky. Do you use salary cost or the full

PM TECHNIQUES

cost of employing that person, which usually works out at roughly double salary? How many days does your organization reckon as a working year. This will not be 365, but will knock off weekends, holidays, and make some allowance for training and sick absence. The figure is usually between 210 and 220. Speak to your finance section if you don't know what your organization does.

If you are employing someone from outside then you will need to agree a contract with them, which will state the payment terms alongside what you want them to do. This may be a flat fee for a piece of work (fixed price), or a day rate (time and materials), usually capped at a set limit. Either way you will know how much to estimate for them.

Equipment costs should also be straightforward – the price to buy or hire what you need. This might also include things like printing costs, or postage. Don't forget to allow for any consumables, such as bar-code labels or floppy disks. Also include an element for maintenance costs if your project will last more than a few weeks. Ten per cent of the original purchase price over a year is the usual figure.

Finally **expenses**. This should include any travel and subsistence – perhaps to interview users in the Outer Hebrides! Again your organization will have rules about what they pay – actuals or a set rate – which will help here. The contract with your external consultants should also set a limit on how much of their expenses you are prepared to pay.

VAT

And don't forget VAT. It is best to account for VAT as a separate element. Some costs – such as your internal staff costs – are likely to be VAT free. But beware, consultants usually charge VAT on top of the quoted fee. If your organization is registered for VAT you may be able to claim some of the money back, but there again... The whole area of VAT is very complex, and again you need to seek guidance from your finance section.

Profiling

Costing is the difficult bit. Having done that, constructing the profile is fairly mechanical. Look at the plan and work out what will be spent when. This gives you a figure against which to monitor what you actually do spend. Remember, though, the difference between when bills are presented and when the money goes out of your budget. To be accurate you should work on the second figure, so you need to know how quickly your organization pays its bills! This is particularly important at the end of the financial year, where in the public sector at least, money not spent may be lost.

The main purpose of the budget profile is to help monitor spend. And for this you will usually want to know:

➤ the total actual spend against what was planned across the period and
➤ actual vs. planned for the individual elements.

This can be done manually as a table. But it is easiest to do it on a spreadsheet which then allows you to create graphs which will help you see what is happening and impress the project board. Total spend is usually a line graph, while individual elements are usually bar graphs.

So, for our User Survey project, if we assume that Fred costs £300 per day, Jane and May £200 each and Bill £100, that printing and postage to send out the questionnaires comes to £50, and hire of equipment for the presentation £25, with another £15 for refreshments for the project board, our budget profile (remembering to allow for a month between commitment and spend) might look like the one shown in Table 5.1.

Table 5.1 Budget profile

	April	May	June
People	1700	250	4600
Equipment	50	0	25
Expenses	0	0	15
Total	1750	250	4640

Then, if the slippage on testing the questionnaire did happen the graph of actual vs. planned might look like the one shown in Figure 5.3.

PM TECHNIQUES

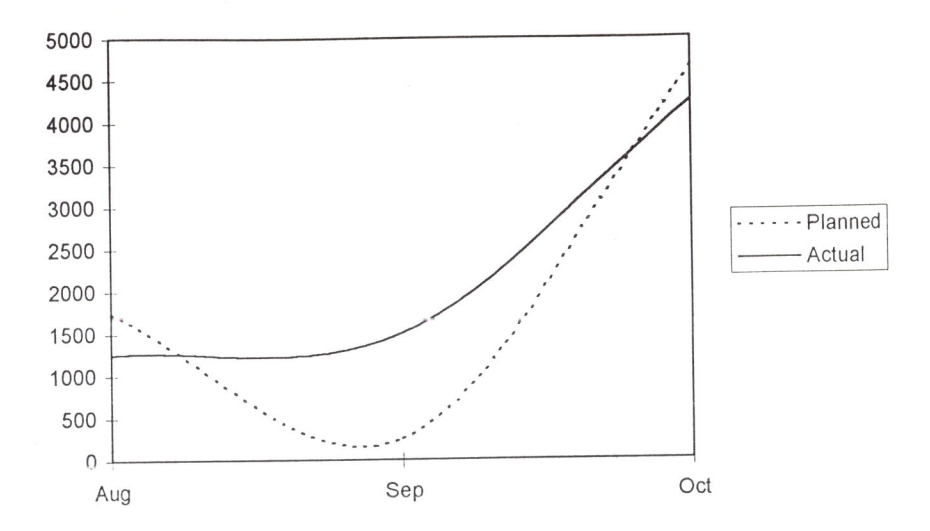

Fig. 5.3 *Spend vs budget for the User Survey*

Could it have been prevented? The last technique we need to look at in this chapter is risk – how to identify what might go wrong.

Risk analysis

In every human activity there is risk – and your project is no different. But if you think in advance about what could go wrong, you are more likely to spot problems early, before they have too devastating an effect on the outcome of the project. Risk analysis makes you think hard about all the aspects of your project, and helps you to identify where things are most likely to go wrong. Most risk analysis is based on a checklist approach – again your organization may have a preferred methodology, and if so you should follow it.

In the sort of projects we are likely to find in a library environment risks come from four main areas:

➤ project management,
➤ project staff,
➤ the nature of the project itself and,
➤ the organization's culture and expectations.

Making project management work for you

Project management

Here you are trying to gauge how well the project is organized, and the most important question is: is the project manager experienced or not? An experienced project manager will know what works and what does not. But everyone has to start somewhere, and a project is not doomed because this is the first project the manager has handled. However, if this is the case, some additional support, perhaps from a more experience manager or from the project board, would be sensible to offset the risk.

Another risk factor in this area is whether or not the project manager is full-time. If the project is small, and particularly if you have employed a project manager from outside your organization, there may not be enough work to justify a full-time manager. He or she may be running several projects at the same time – and this can work perfectly well. However, there is a risk when sharing resources that your project manager will not be available when you need them.

Project staff

The same of course can be true of other members of the project team. How experienced are the members of the team and how up-to-date is their knowledge and skill set? Do you need to build in additional time for training?

Wherever staff have other duties there is the risk of a clash of priorities, and the danger that your project will lose out. Staff turnover can also be a major risk factor. On short projects it may not matter too much, unless you are very unlucky. But if the project will last several months or years there is a risk that one or more member will leave the team and there will be a delay while you recruit new project staff and bring them up to speed.

The level of involvement of project staff with the outcome of the project is important too. If the project will directly affect their future work then success is in their interests and you can expect a high level of informed commitment. If not, then you need to make sure that you actively involve the people who will be affected to make sure that you are producing a result that they actually want.

PM TECHNIQUES

The nature of the project itself

Of course the most risky area is the nature of the project itself. New projects are more risky than ones which have been done before and where procedures have been tested. Projects under your immediate control are less risky than those at a distance which you can only visit from time to time. Stand alone projects are less risky than those which depend for their success on the completion to time of other projects outside the immediate control of the project manager. The project to move the books from British Library sites around London cannot complete until the St Pancras building is accepted and ready to receive them.

Short projects are less risky than long ones, when staff can move or ideas on what the project is to deliver can change. Any project which involves the use of IT is particularly constrained – the pace of development is so rapid that top of the range equipment bought two years ago is now not powerful enough to run current software.

Projects which impact upon the business of the organization are risky. Our second example – the Loans System – is risky because if it fails or is late the library will not be able to lend books at the start of the new term. And if things go very badly wrong users might not even be able to get into the building! The more people the project affects the higher the level of risk.

Projects which have to be completed by a certain date are risky. All projects have a tendency to slip and if the end date cannot move there will be additional pressure to try to complete on time. Pressure in itself is risky because it can lead to actions which are not properly thought out and whose outcomes are uncertain.

Where you need to buy things, the track record of the supplier is important. A well-established supplier for whom your order is one of a number of similar size is less risky than a newcomer to the business, or a sole trader or one where your order is significantly bigger or more complex than any previous supply.

The nature and experience of the organization

And finally the nature of the organization, and how it manages projects affects the likelihood of a successful outcome. Already, in several previous chapters, I have said, 'Find out what standards your organization works to and use these.' An organization which is used to running projects and which has a well-defined set of standards and methodologies is less risky than one which does not. It will save time, and give you as project manager more confidence, if you can follow a well-understood procedure for, say, quality review. And a project which runs into difficulties is much more likely to overcome them if the project manager knows when the limit of his or her authority is reached and where to go for help. Projects which go disastrously wrong usually do so because someone tries to cover up an original mistake, or to put things right before anybody notices – look at Barings Bank!

How to calculate risk

Risk checklists usually comprise lists of pairs of statements – one signifying low risk, the other high – with a scale between them. Most organizations have their own checklists, but if not CCTA have a very useful *Risk management checklist for IT projects* which can be adapted for other types of project, and which is the basis for Table 5.2 below. Even if you are using a standard list you should still consider whether there are any risks which are particular to your project – you will already have thought about this in your project plan – and add them in. For each statement you need to consider:

➤ where on the scale your project sits;
➤ how important that factor is to your project, again on a scale

and allocate a number to each. Multiplying the two numbers together, then adding up all the results will give the risk score for your project.

You can then work out low and high limits for the project by adding up all the figures in the weight column and multiplying the total by, say, 2 for low risk and 3 for high. Comparing your score with these limits will tell you whether the overall project is low, medium or high risk. Table 5.2 shows how to do this for the Loans System project.

Table 5.2 Risk checklist

Low risk	Scale	High risk	Weight	Total
	1 2 3 4		3 4 5 6	
Full-time experienced project manager	1	Inexperienced or part-time project manager	5	5
Project team is experienced and has appropriate skills	2	Team is inexperienced and lack the appropriate skills	3	6
Staff are dedicated to the project	3	Staff have other duties	4	12
Installation of a system which has been used elsewhere	1	Installation of a new system	3	3
Business will not be affected	4	Significant impact on business operations	5	20
Little or no modification or development work undertaken	2	Extensive modification or development needed	3	6
Little constraint on completion date	4	Mandatory completion date	4	16
Suppliers are well-established and experienced	2	Suppliers are new or one-man businesses	2	4
Few users	4	Many users	4	16
No dependence on other projects outside manager's control	3	Heavy dependence on other projects outside manager's control	5	15
Well-developed set of standards and procedures in use	1	Few or no standards and procedures in use	3	3
Delegation of authority is clear	1	Delegation of authority is not clear	3	3
Totals	28		44	109

Low risk if score less than 2 × weight = 88
High risk if score is greater than 3 × weight = 132
Project is therefore **medium** risk = 109

The risk score will help you to decide what the likelihood of success for your project is. If it looks too risky it may not be worth starting. It certainly is worth looking at again to see what you can do to minimize the risks. If the risk score is very low perhaps you have been too pessimistic in your estimates and you could do it faster, or with fewer resources.

However the major benefit of risk analysis comes from looking at the items with high values – 3s or 4s – in the risk scale. These are the elements that you have identified as being risky – so they are the ones to pay particular attention to during the project. In this example the project has been done before elsewhere, the team are experienced and the organization has well-established procedures. These are low risks. However the deadline is fixed, there are external dependencies (in this case delivery of the bar-codes and completing the accommodation changes) and the impact on the library's business is great. Making sure that everything happens on time and querying any delay will be critical to the success of the project. Also the staff have other duties, which might call them away at critical parts of the project. Making sure that everyone knows when they are needed and establishing good communication with other managers will also be important.

So, undertaking a risk analysis helps you as project manager to establish your priorities, and shows you where the dangerous areas are. We will cover what to do with this information in Chapter 7 'What To Do When Things Go Wrong'.

To sum up

In this chapter we have looked at the formal aspect of project management techniques. We have learned about:

➤ **GANTT (or bar) charts**
➤ **critical path method**
➤ **PERT (or flow) charts**
➤ **network analysis and**
➤ **risk analysis**

and when and how to use them.

In the next chapter we will look at putting all of this to use, Implementing the Project.

Chapter 6
Implementing the project

> In this chapter we will see how to bring all of this together. It will cover
>
> ➤ doing the job – turning the plan into action
> ➤ monitoring – making sure that things are going OK
> ➤ dealing with change
> ➤ completing the project.

With a good plan you are well on the way to success. However planning and doing are different things and projects do not run themselves. It is very easy once you are deep into the day-to-day activity of the project, to forget all about the plan and start reacting to events as they occur. This is particularly true when things go wrong. So implementing the project is not just a matter of doing the job, but also of keeping a close eye on the plan, monitoring where you are against where you ought to be, keeping the team motivated, keeping everybody involved informed and making sure the budget is on track. You may well feel like a circus plate spinner, running up and down the line trying to keep all those plates on their vibrating poles!

Doing the job

The plan tells you what tasks or activities need to be done by whom, when and in what order. But this is still at quite a high level. It does not tell you how to do the tasks, or exactly what to do. Now you and your project team need to break each task down into sub-tasks – what needs to be done and how to do it.

Let's look back at the User Survey. One of the early tasks is to *select recipients* of the questionnaire. The entire project team is down for this one. So what needs to be done? The first thing is to decide how many people are needed for a representative sample. 20? 30? 5%? 10%? You need enough to give a credible result, but also not so many that you cannot cope with the numbers. The next task is to identify the actual respondents. How to choose? Perhaps everyone suggests names of people they know – but this would bias the result by excluding non-users. Or perhaps names are selected at random, every tenth or twentieth name from the college database. Whatever method you choose will affect the result, and will also have a knock-on effect on the task itself.

Each task therefore needs to be broken down into the individual activities that will complete it. These activities will be very practical – phone computer section to ask for print-out, check availability of computer to analyse results, book lecture hall for date of presentation – rather than the high level which is appropriate for the plan. They become in effect a checklist for the individual team members of the things they need to do to complete their part of the project.

When you have assigned responsibility for a task to someone else it is reasonable to expect them to get on and do it. However you do need to make sure that what they are doing fits in with the rest of the project, in other words that the quality is right. Choosing the first 50 people from the college list may give the right number and be a quick and easy method. But if the list is sorted by category, with staff first, the sample will not be representative. This is where the standards or the success factors set out in the quality plan are useful in helping you, as project manager, to see whether the way in which the task is to be carried out will actually deliver what you want.

Which brings us on to . . .

Monitoring

Unless your project is very small, and you are carrying it out single-handed, you can assume that most of the doing will be up to your team. As project manager your main task in this stage is monitoring progress against the plan. We looked in the last chapter at the use of GANTT charts and budget control charts as techniques to use in monitoring. The next chapter What To Do When Things Go Wrong will cover in detail what to look out for, and the options that you have. In this chapter we need to discuss **how** to monitor.

Implementing the project

There are three main areas, like the legs of a stool, which need to be kept in balance for the project to proceed to a completely successful conclusion:

➤ timescale – is the project proceeding to plan, will it be completed on time;
➤ quality – do the results of each stage match the success factors, will the project achieve its objective;
➤ budget – are the costs under control, will the project come in on or below budget.

We have already looked at monitoring the budget in the last chapter, so let's consider timescale and quality.

Timescale

There are two main ways of monitoring progress – meetings and reports which we looked at in Chapter 3 'Project organization'. **Checkpoint meetings** with the whole team are important in keeping everybody up-to-date on what is happening and maintaining momentum. The meetings should be regular, every week if possible, but should not be too long – half-an-hour to an hour is usually enough. They should cover:

➤ achievements, what has been done in the period since the last meeting; this can be done either through written reports circulated in advance or verbally, depending on the scale of the project;
➤ next tasks, what is the workplan for the next period;
➤ issues, what has happened (or is likely to happen) that might affect progress on the project;
➤ budget, what has been spent. Detailed reports on spend are best handled on paper in advance, with a summary report to the meeting. But it is important for the team as well as the project board to know how the budget is going.

These meetings serve a number of purposes. As well as providing you with the information you need to compare actual progress against the plan they also help to keep the team informed and motivated. The progress reports keep everyone up to speed on where the others are in

55

their part of the plan, and what they will be doing next. Thinking through issues flushes out possible problems early – so minimizing the unpleasant surprises – and gets everyone involved in trying to solve them.

After each meeting you should produce a **checkpoint report** for the benefit of the team, to record what was discussed and agreed. These will form the basis of the **highlight reports** which you will produce, usually at longer intervals, for the project board. They will also feed into the information that you give out to the wider community – users, colleagues etc.

Quality

We looked at success factors and drew up a list of deliverables in Chapter 4 Planning the Project. In implementing the project you will actually be producing these deliverables – in our example things like the results of the test questionnaire or the outline analysis method. You need to check that they are what you expected, and you do this through **quality review**.

When you drew up the quality plan you identified for each deliverable who should look at it and what criteria they should assess it against. The reviewer should not be the person who produced the deliverable, and where possible you should have more than one reviewer so that you get different viewpoints. The project manager will usually read everything, and will also make full use of the project assurance team. Where the deliverable is a report recommending action it is useful to have one reviewer who is not part of the project team. This ensures that the recommendations are logical, and flow from the evidence presented.

How you collect comments is up to you. But written comments are better than verbal, a separate document is better than marginal notes and best of all is a review sheet which indicates:

➤ where the comment is (page, paragraph or even line numbers really help here);
➤ the comment – problems or additional information;
➤ ideas on what actions might help resolve any problems;

➤ the severity of the comment – high, medium or low. Identifying a problem which would cause the project to fail is of a different order to a comment on presentation.

Reviews in this form really help the originator of the deliverable and the project manager to improve the next draft. When the reviewers agree that the deliverable is OK it should be formally accepted, either by the project manager or the board depending on its importance.

Take care with final reports which are made up from reports on earlier stages. This is quite common in library projects. The user survey report would have sections on the methodology adopted, selection method for recipients, report on the test questionnaire, analysis method and findings as well as conclusions and recommendations. Putting the final report together is not just a matter of using the merge function in your word processor. Each chapter should be reviewed not just for its own quality but also for its contribution to the overall report.

Dealing with change

No project ever goes completely to plan and yours will not be the first. At some point you will need to manage a change from what you expected. The rules for managing change in projects are the same as elsewhere:

➤ spot problems early;
➤ identify options distinctly;
➤ decide on the appropriate action quickly;
➤ communicate the change clearly.

We will be looking in the next chapter at how to spot problems and the options open to you. Remember, however, that you have others to help you. Create an atmosphere which allows team members to let you know as soon as something seems to be not quite right. Ask questions in the checkpoint meetings. Discuss options with your team and with suppliers if appropriate. Problems are rarely completely new and other people's experience is valuable.

With a small-scale project you can probably implement a change on your own authority. But with larger projects you may need to get the project board's approval. They will want a very clear picture of the problem, its seriousness, all the available options with their implications not only for your project but also any other projects and the rest of the organization. The project board's job is to take the wider view of the project and may have different preferences as a result. Delaying part of the loans system might get you out of a hole, but if it meant that committed budget savings could not be made the project board might decide to press ahead.

Once the change has been agreed and approved you should document it and revise the plan. Remember to give the new plan an updated version number so that everyone can keep track. Then communicate the changes to everyone involved, including users etc. outside the team if the change will affect them. If you need to change an order to a supplier or contractor you may need to issue a formal change request, so that they can adjust their plans and documentation. Always ask them for written confirmation of the change to avoid arguments later. In larger projects, especially those with a high IT content changes will be numbered, and a list kept.

Completion

As you come towards the end of the project there is a natural tendency for the pressure to relax. The fun part of planning and doing is over and only the boring part of writing-up is left. Your responsibility as project manager is not over until all the reports are completed and signed off and the project is formally closed. If you don't want to be up till four in the morning tying up the loose ends make sure you keep your team motivated right up to the end.

Once the main work is over there may be some tidying up to do. If you have hired equipment for the project you will need to send it back. If you have occupied special accommodation you will need to move yourselves (and assorted clutter) out. And if staff have been specially assigned to the project they will need to find (or be found) other jobs. Don't forget to put the project documentation into order. The project manager of the next stage will not thank you for six boxes of loose paper!

IMPLEMENTING THE PROJECT

Your organization may have particular procedures to follow in closing projects (in PRINCE it is a business acceptance letter). Usually this will be a document which agrees that the project has delivered what was agreed (as modified by changes along the way) and which signs off the result. Sometimes formal acceptance is delayed until after the project review – a subject we will look at in Chapter 8 – and sometimes not.

Having done all that it's time to party!

To sum up

Implementing the project is more than just doing the job. In this chapter we have looked at:

➤ **how to turn the plan into action**
➤ **what monitoring means**
➤ **how to manage the inevitable changes and**
➤ **what to do at the end of the project.**

Before we get carried away let's have a look at what can go wrong, and what to do about it.

Chapter 7
What to do when things go wrong

> Projects do not always go according to plan. This chapter will tell you:
> ➤ what to look for
> ➤ how to spot the danger signs
> ➤ and what you can do about them.

That great project manager Murphy states in his first three Laws:

➤ If a thing can go wrong, it will.
➤ When things can't get worse, they will.
➤ If all is going well you have forgotten something.

Your project will not go according to plan. Vital equipment will be late, a key team member will be unavailable at the most inconvenient point, a task will prove more complex, take twice as long and cost three times as much as you thought it would. One report in 1987 found that of 3000 public sector projects 95% overran on time, or budget, or both – and more recent surveys suggest things have not changed.

In Chapters 2 and 5 we have looked at what you can do to minimize the likelihood of things going wrong – writing down the assumptions you are making and thinking through what might go wrong. In the implementation stage monitoring becomes one of the project manager's main tasks. Spotting problems early is the key to putting them right and to avoiding being the disaster quoted in all the textbooks. So what sort of things do we need to look for?

Think back to the three legs to our project discussed in the last chapter – timescale, quality and budget. For each area you need to know how each of them is going. When they start to diverge from the plan you need to know:

WHAT TO DO WHEN THINGS GO WRONG

➤ that it is happening;
➤ what impact the divergence will have on the overall project; and
➤ what options you have to correct it.

How to spot problems

Regular monitoring is essential to successful project management. Your risk analysis will have helped you to see where some of the danger might lie, and you should pay particular attention to the high risk areas. But problems have a habit of coming where you least expect them. The earlier you know that something has not gone according to plan the more you can do about it. When things start to go wrong you need to know quickly what has happened and why. There are certain danger signals to watch out for.

Slipping timescales

Is the project up to schedule? Is each task being done on time? In Chapter 5 we looked at GANTT charts, and how they could be used to keep track of how close each task was to completion. In that example one task was late, and this would impact on all the others. Timescales can slip for a number of reasons.

A supplier may not deliver equipment when promised or a contractor may fail to meet the deadline you agreed. In the Loans System example the project timescale depends on the bar-code labels being delivered and on new power points being installed on time. If your supplier's factory burns down, or the power points job gets missed off the electrician's rota, you have a problem. Both dependencies are outside your control as project manager, and so you will need to check with those responsible to make sure that all is well.

A task may be more difficult, or may need more people, than you thought. You might have estimated the duration for bar-coding the books at a rate of 50 per person per hour. But perhaps a high proportion of your books have shiny covers, and the bar codes won't stick – so one person can only do 25 books in an hour. The duration of the task has doubled. If you have not done a task before you need to check your assumptions on how long it will take.

61

The consequence of slippage is to put more pressure onto the project. Later non-critical tasks lose their flexibility and any slack disappears. Desirable tasks, which might have found windows of opportunity, are jettisoned. And missed deadlines will have a knock-on effect on the rest of the project. If the bar-coding is late the dependent task to load copy and title information onto the loans system cannot start on time. If contract staff were being used to do the loading and they are only available for a particular period (perhaps you are using students during vacation) then that task may not be able to complete, and the whole project is in danger.

So keep a close eye on the timescale of the tasks in your plan. Are deadlines being met? Is progress up to schedule?

Poor quality

Checking progress against the plan should enable you to see if the timescale is on track. However a project may complete on time, but still fail to achieve its objective because of poor quality. Quality is a more difficult element to monitor, because problems may not be so immediately obvious. This is especially true if you are working in an area where you are not expert and are dependent on others for vital elements. How will you know whether what they have delivered is of the appropriate quality?

This can be an issue for libraries in installing small-scale computer systems for library housekeeping which need to integrate with an existing organization-wide IT infrastructure. Many people find it hard to specify what they want until they know what the system can do, and the system cannot be built until the specification is clear. If you want to generate a new accessions list from the catalogue and put it directly onto the office bulletin board you need an output format which, say, sorts by author within subject, separates headings, authors, titles and location details and applies a style to each. System designers are not mind-readers, and unless you specify to that level of detail you may end up with an undifferentiated block of text to edit. Good communication about the objectives of the project and a clear specification or quality standard are essential.

What to do when things go wrong

The best way to measure quality is against criteria agreed at the start. In some cases this is easy. If you set a maximum period for the Loans System to find a book from its bar-code of five seconds and it takes ten then that part of the system has failed. If you set a critical success factor of 60% questionnaires returned for the User Survey and you only get 20% then the survey is invalid and project itself has failed.

It is more difficult to set criteria where analysis and interpretation are involved. Is the report from the User Survey good or bad? Referring back to the objective of the project is useful here. If the report helps the librarian to see what needs to be done to meet the expressed requirements of the users it has achieved its objective. If not, not.

However, remember that quality means 'fitness for purpose'. Perhaps 20% is a perfectly adequate sample size, and to go for 60% would extend the project by three weeks and cost another £500. 'Good enough' is exactly that. Do not allow perfectionism to distort your project.

Over (or under) budget

When planning the project in Chapter 4 we set a budget profile – how much money we expected to pay when and to whom. Monitoring the budget is superficially quite easy. Compare the actual spend with the planned spend and note any divergence.

Overspending is an obvious problem – you are in danger of running out of money to pay for the project and you need to do something **now**! But underspending can also be a danger signal. It may be that you were too pessimistic in your cost calculations, but it is more likely that the underspend is the result of work not being done or goods not delivered.

However, even if the actual spend is what you expected the project may still be in trouble. Budget, quality and timescale are all related. If the timescale is slipping tasks may be building up for later, when the budget has run out. If the quality is poor more time and money may be needed to put it right.

What to do when things go wrong

Once you have identified what has gone wrong the next questions to ask are – why did it go wrong and does it matter?

63

The bar-codes being late because of a one-day postal strike is on a different scale from the factory burning down. Once you know the reason for the problem you can assess how far it will affect the successful completion of the project as a whole. Review the plan. How long will it take to resolve the problem? Is there any slack you can call upon in the timescale? Can some tasks be brought forward to use dead time? If a supplier has failed can an alternative be delivered within the time? Is there any unallocated money in the budget to absorb the change? If a contractor has caused the problem can you get them to pay? Often it is possible to resolve problems and keep the project on course by replanning. Don't forget to involve your team in this replanning – they may well be able to see a solution that you can't!

Try not to apportion blame. All too often, when problems occur time is wasted trying to decide whose fault it was rather than sorting the problem out. What tends to happen is that people adopt defensive positions, which will make it more difficult to understand what went wrong and why. This does not mean that you should not assign responsibility. If a problem occurred because a team member did not complete a task as agreed they must take that responsibility. If a supplier failed to deliver materials when they were due they should bear the financial consequences as set out in the contract. But an atmosphere where all parties are prepared to acknowledge early that they have made a mistake will get the project back on track much more quickly than one where everyone is covering their backs.

If, once you have replanned, you find that you will exceed your tolerance on time and/or your contingency on budget you need to consider what options you have. These are:

➤ change the timescale;
➤ change what you do (scope, objectives, quality);
➤ change what resources you use (people/budget);
➤ stop the project.

Change the timescale

Timescale is the most likely element to be flexible. Does the project have to be finished by a particular date? If the Queen is coming to open your

WHAT TO DO WHEN THINGS GO WRONG

new library the answer is probably yes. The Loans System is timed to be operational by the start of the new term – not much flexibility on timing there. But if the date is arbitrary you could negotiate an extension – the presentation for the User Survey could take place after the Chief Executive gets back from holiday.

Perhaps you could omit some stages to speed up implementation. In the User Survey you could miss out testing the questionnaire and save five days. Or perhaps you could phase the implementation, delivering some of the project now and some later on when you might have more resources.

Change the scope/quality (objectives)

If the timescale is fixed, perhaps you can change the scope of the project. Look back at the original criteria set up when you defined the project, drop the desirables and nice-to-haves and focus on the essentials. In the Loans System the scope originally covered all loanable stock, including maps. Let us assume that books have the heaviest use in this library. The project could concentrate on these, and on current serials as they came in. Older serials and maps could be loaded as they were issued once term began. By changing the scope you can allow for a phased implementation which will allow the project to complete over a longer timescale.

Also have a look at quality. Is the standard set too high? Are you a special library with a heavy emphasis on immediate information and are you cataloguing to AACR2 level 3? Could the project be completed, and the essential objectives achieved if lower standards were adopted?

Change the resources (people/budget)

The third option is to put in more resources into the project. If your project has high prestige and it simply must succeed this is a viable option. You may be able to move staff from lower priority tasks onto your project, or even to allocate additional budget. However be prepared for hard questions to be asked by your managers about why the extra resources are needed and how confident you are that the additional funds will ensure success. Beware of making statements like

65

'The project is practically finished.'
'We just have a few teething problems.'
'It's not my fault.'

There are many well-documented disasters, such as the London Stock Exchange Taurus system for automated share settlements or the London Ambulance Service computer-aided despatch system, where extra resources could not offset poor project management, the costs escalated alarmingly and the project still failed.

Stop the project

Stopping the project may seem to be an admission of failure, but sometimes it is worse to carry on. A spectacular failure can be more damaging to future projects (and to your reputation as a project manager) than stopping in a rational and tidy manner. A report which documents what went wrong and can be invaluable to a new team. You should consider this option if:

➤ things have gone so badly wrong that you have no realistic chance of achieving your objective;
➤ it would cost too much to put the project back on track;
➤ circumstances have changed and the project is no longer needed.

Even if things are not quite at this pass it can be sensible to put the project on hold while you work out what to do next.

One word of caution. If you are considering cancellation remember to check what your commitments are. If you have a contract with suppliers you may not be able to save as much as you expect.

Exception reports

Whenever you depart significantly from your plan you need to let the Project Board know what has happened, why, what you are doing about it and what the impact on the rest of the project will be in an exception report. If you are asking for longer to complete the project, or a change in scope, or more money or permission to stop you must give the project board the opportunity to review what has happened and to decide whether or not the project should continue. In this way responsibility is

WHAT TO DO WHEN THINGS GO WRONG

rightly shared between you as project manager and the people who are ultimately responsible for the project's success or failure.

However . . .

Remember that, despite the headlines, many, many projects succeed. Think of the Apollo space rockets, or the Tate Gallery at St Ives or, perhaps in a few years' time, the new British Library!

To sum up

In this chapter we have discussed monitoring. We have covered:

- the danger signs when things are going wrong
- the need for rapid assessment of what, why and how important
- what the options are to deal with the situation
- getting the Board's agreement.

Well, the project is finished. Was it a success or a failure? In the next chapter we look at Evaluation.

Chapter 8
Evaluation

> At the end of the project it is important to look back and see:
> - was the project a success or not?
> - how could you have done better?
> - what have you learned about your environment for the future?

The project is finished. You've had the party. So, how did it go and what have you learned? All too often project managers (and project boards) are so relieved to have got to the end of the project without major mishap that the evaluation stage is missed out. This is a pity, because a thorough and honest evaluation is a vital part of improving skills, both for the project manager and the organization. Every project is different, even if it is similar to previous projects, and there is always something to be learned from what happened.

Organizations have different approaches to project evaluation. But most will carry out some form of post-project review, usually on all their projects above a certain financial threshold but also on a percentage of smaller projects. Even if you do not do a formal report, it is well worth writing down the lessons learned for your own future use.

Was it a success or a failure?

Deciding whether a project was a success or a failure is not as easy as it sounds. Let's look at the Channel Tunnel. The project was very complex, and there were numerous disputes between Eurotunnel and the contractors. It was two years late in completion, and is so far over budget that it is hard to see it ever repaying the debt. But it is a magnificent piece of engineering and was immediately popular with passengers. Within the first year of operation it had captured a large part of the freight business. Is it a success or a failure?

EVALUATION

Success or failure can depend on your point of view. The Loans System project will be a success for the Senior Technical on the project board if the system installation went smoothly and if the loans module integrates well with the OPAC. Senior Finance will be happy if it came in on (or preferably below) budget. The users will be pleased if it allows them to borrow and reserve material more quickly. But if only part of the stock was loaded, and as a result the system cannot deliver management information on stock usage the Senior User will not be content. And if the problems which caused delay on the project disrupted other work in the library because additional staff were drafted, in the Chair may well see the project as only partially successful.

How do you measure success?

Wherever possible it is best to look for objective measures when evaluating the success of the project. At this stage we are looking as far as possible at yes/no answers. And that is why it is so important to have clear objectives and a good plan at the start, and why changes to the plan should be recorded. That way you can tell much more easily whether the project achieved what was intended. Let's look at some objective measures.

Was it on time?

This is pretty unambiguous! If the project was due to complete on a particular date did it or didn't it? Where the timescale has been adjusted, either to lengthen or shorten it, then this final date is the one you should go by **provided that** the change was properly documented, agreed by the project board and the plans updated to show the new date.

Was it within budget?

Again this should be quite clear. When doing the initial cost-benefit analysis you should have included all the costs which would fall to the project, and allowed a certain level of contingency for the unexpected. Are you above or below the line? Make sure, when you are making up the final account for the cost element that you have included all the commitments as well as the actual money spent. Sometimes suppliers can be slow in presenting bills. Watch out also for extra costs incurred because of problems outside the project's control. Should these rightly fall to the project or to the agent which caused the problem?

Was the quality right?

Were the deliverables or outputs of the project actually up to the standard set in the quality plan? Could the recipients of the questionnaire understand what they were being asked? Did the completed forms give a clear picture of what the users thought? Were the responses on the loans module within the limits set down in the specification?

Did it deliver the required benefits?

With long or complex projects it can be easy to forget what you were trying to achieve in the first place. That is why it is so important, when you are defining the project, to set out what your objectives are, and when you are planning to think about those critical success factors. How did we score? The library was open for business on the first day of term, all the borrower records were on, and the short loan collection and the current serials. All the essentials and a couple of the desirables. Pretty good!

In thinking about the benefits delivered, remember all the benefits over time. The User Survey benefits are short-term and self contained – informing the new librarian about what the users think of the library. Subsequent action taken to improve the service will be a new project, and the benefits will count to that project not to this. The Loans System is a longer-term project. The benefits in improved staff efficiency and user satisfaction should occur over several years. You may need to do a follow-up review after a year to see if the system is still performing and delivering the benefits as planned.

What could you have done better?

Deciding on how successful (or not) the project was may grab the headlines, but it is the least useful part of the evaluation. Much more important is the analysis of what worked and what didn't. What went wrong and why. To be truly valuable this has to be honest – you cannot learn from your mistakes unless you acknowledge what they were. What really went wrong? Why did it happen and how could it have been avoided? Focus on the key areas of the project. This will not help the current project – but it can give invaluable information for the next one!

Were the **objectives** of the project realistic? Or were you really trying to do more than was possible? Perhaps it was always an outside chance that all the loan stock would be loaded onto the system, and it would have caused less stress to the team if they had focused on the high-use material first. Realism in defining and scoping is perhaps the most valuable lesson to be learned from past projects. One of the most common causes of project failure is an over-ambitious, ill-thought-out or poorly understood specification.

How about the **communication**, both inside the team and with others? This is another frequent cause of project failure. Were tasks not carried out because there was confusion about who was supposed to be dealing with them? Did you assume that 'any right-thinking person would realize that' . . . the high-use stock needed to be done before the rest, or that the books needed to be recalled well before the end of term? And perhaps the stiff letter from the teaching staff could have been avoided if you had given them a timetable of opening hours.

How was the **timing**? Did the bar-code labels have a six-week lead time rather than four? Had you allowed for the shiny covers slowing down the labelling process? Was the team sitting on its hands because a task had completed early? At the end of the project you know how long tasks actually took, so have a better idea of real durations for the future.

Were important stages missed out? Did the User Survey questionnaire not work properly because it was not tested first? Did you forget to ask for a site inspection by the electricians before they installed the power points? (One university library did forget this when planning its new extension, and the power points ended up in front of the enquiry desk, where the readers stood.) Now you have a better idea of **scheduling**, and what sort of tasks are likely to be dependent on others.

Did you have the right **resources**? In the end were there enough vacation students to do the bar-coding? Did your team have the right skills? Was the reason that the questionnaire went wrong because Mary had never done one before and Jane left her to it? Did you allocate them correctly, or did you forget to consult Bill's line manager and found too late that he could not be released?

What about the **budget**? Were the assumptions about how much things would cost accurate, and did the costs fall when you expected them to? Did you remember to include VAT on the contractors bills? Can what you have learned about timing and scheduling help you to make better estimates of the money needed, and profile spend more accurately? For many organizations coming in on or below budget is the most important factor in judging the success (or lack) of a project – and of you as a project manager.

But, don't forget to look also at **what went well**. The newsletter that was particularly good in keeping everyone informed. The way that the team worked together and helped each other. How easy that piece of software made it for you to get just the names you needed for the User Survey. How well the second supplier performed when you needed barcodes in a hurry. As well as saying thank you, remember what worked well. So that you can do it again.

What have you learned about your environment?

As well as the immediate lessons on project management (how to do it better) each project also teaches you about your environment. Who was the most useful person you came across during the project, who understood what you were trying to do and helped you? That person could well be an ally for future projects. Was anyone unhelpful, or even obstructive? Why? You may need to spend more time understanding their concerns if you are to gain their support.

What is the most effective way to get things done in the organization – the usual route may be through A, but B worked better and faster. Projects can teach you a lot about how organizations **really** work, as opposed to how they say they do.

How did your team members perform? Perhaps you expected a lot of Jane, but she let you down. Whereas Mary, with relatively little experience, really got her teeth into the project and performed well. Working in a project tests not only your staff's professional skills, but also their potential for other jobs.

EVALUATION

This is not the sort of information gathered from, or put into, the evaluation report on a project. It is more likely to emerge towards the end of the post-project session in the pub, where the team feel free to talk about their experiences. Projects are about achieving your objective in the most cost-effective manner. Learning as much as you can about what happened in this one will give you a head start on the next.

And so on to the next one

And the last thing to cover in the post-project evaluation is the **next** project. What has the project recommended about the way forward? The User Survey will not be the end – the librarian will need to act on the results, and this will lead to new projects. The Loans module will provide the management information for further work to maximize stock efficiency.

Using a project management approach to for the whole library lets you plan the development of your service. It allows you to see which project should come first, and how best to use the staff and other resources at your disposal. At the individual level it helps you to make best use of your time, and so to achieve more.

To sum up

In this chapter we have looked at:

➤ **how to measure success**
➤ **how to learn from your mistakes . . .**
➤ **. . . and your successes**
➤ **what to build on for the future.**

That's this project finished. But in the real world you are likely to have more than one project on at a time. In the last chapter we look at multiple projects, and how project management software can help.

73

Chapter 9
The real world – multiple projects

> Up to now we have been looking at how to manage a single project. But projects, like the number 11 bus, come altogether or not at all. In this chapter we will look at:
>
> ➤ using project management to get things done
> ➤ what to look out for in managing multiple projects
> ➤ how project management software can help.

On a scale of 1 to 10 managing one project is 1, two projects is 3, three projects is 6 and four projects is 32!

Getting things done

Managing multiple projects is more difficult, but with a good understanding of the techniques of project management five, ten or more projects can be managed at once. And, once it becomes a way of life, then your entire job can become much more manageable. Very few managers at whatever level have just one area of responsibility, or a single task to carry through. It is all too easy for managers to miss deadlines or to lose important opportunities to develop the service because they are bound to the in-tray or the enquiry desk.

The techniques of project management – defining, planning, monitoring and evaluating – are closely allied to time management. Used together with a business plan they can help to manage the complexity of today's library, to step back from the urgent and to see the important. This is more productive for the business and more satisfying for the individual.

If you run your job or your library on a project management basis you will **know** whether you have the resources to take on an extra piece or work. You will be able to tell by looking at your plan where the pressure points are and where there are gaps in the schedule where something new could be slotted in. If one area of work goes wrong you can see what the impact will be on other work. If more resources are needed for the bar-coding you can see if there is any slack in the journal renewals which could be redeployed. And, if you have thought about what could go wrong you will be at less risk from the unexpected. In short you will be **managing** and not **coping** with your job.

However multiple projects have some special features, which we need to look at next.

Multiple projects

First of all are the projects separate or are they stages of the same project? The loans module is a continuation of the public access catalogue project – staff on the first project may have experience which would be useful on the second. Related projects may be dependent, at least in part, on each other. They may have similar milestones and share similar risks. Achieving the objective of extending service to the user population for both the OPAC and the Loans System projects may be dependent on the college extending the network to teaching departments.

In multiple projects scheduling and resource allocation are closely linked. It is likely that all the projects are drawing on the same resource pool. This brings benefits from shared experience, reduced training and easier communication. But staff need guidance on priorities and reporting lines when they are working on more than one project. Shared resources put pressure on a project if a key team member is required for a later project. A clear view of the projects' objectives and good communication between project managers are essential to resolve these sort of conflicts. A single authority or some form of dispute resolution procedure may be necessary.

Monitoring for multiple projects is more complex. You really need a three-dimensional matrix showing all the projects. But to try to do this at the same level of detail would be impossible. One way is to draw up a 'super project' which contains all the other projects in summary and to use this to track progress at the unit or library level. Individual project managers report on progress, focusing on issues which affect other projects. Financial monitoring is probably the least affected and has most to gain. Early warning of an overspend on a high priority project allows for the reallocation of funds from others of less importance.

However planning and monitoring at this level can benefit from the right software.

How project management software can help

Project management software has good and bad points, and you need to think carefully before you make the decision to use it.

Among its **advantages** are the following.

- ▶ It makes updating easier. You set up the relationships between projects and the software works out the relationships and recalculates timescales each time you make a change.
- ▶ Graphical output makes it easier to see what is going on. We have looked in previous chapters at GANTT and PERT charts and have seen how much easier it is to understand both the flow of the project and where you are at any one time.
- ▶ You can track numerous tasks at the same time. Most software will allow you to put in summary tasks and to expand or collapse your view of the GANTT chart depending on what you want. Such flexibility is beyond most mechanical or paper approaches without a Master's degree in origami.
- ▶ You can see when shared resources are in danger of being over-allocated. One of the main strengths of project management software is the control it gives you over the resource pool. You can set up calendars for resources, human and equipment which are individual to them. So you don't need to remember that Bill is on holiday all of February, or the training room is only free on Fridays – the software will do it for you. You can also set a limit on the availability of individuals. If Mary is working on four projects she can only give 25% of her time to yours. When you try to go over these limits the software will alert you to the problem, though unfortunately it will not also sort it out for you.

But there are also **disadvantages**.

The real world – multiple projects

- It is difficult software to learn. In my experience it takes about three months to learn project management software, and about six months to master it. Like other specialized software you need to understand the principles of what you want to do – in this case project management – before you can drive the software.
- It offers so many options that the inexperienced user might miss what is going on. A major benefit is that settings on one table read through to others. So the fact that Mary has only 25% availability for a task that needs a whole week's effort will show up as a problem. But it is easy to get confused about the settings and not to understand what the software is telling you. Interestingly the latest version of one of the market leaders, Microsoft® *Project*, offers fewer options than earlier versions.
- It is expensive to load and maintain all the data necessary for meaningful reports. The software itself can be inexpensive. Although professional packages can run into thousands of pounds PC packages start from as little as £50, while £700 will buy a package which will do all you will ever need, and more. The real cost comes in the time and effort it takes to keep the information up to date. There is no point in setting up a project using the software if you are not then going to record progress and changes to the plan – and this can take a lot of operator time.

Use it when your projects:

- are complex, with many tasks and dependencies; if your GANTT chart goes over a single landscape page of A4 then project management software will probably help;
- have timescales of more than three months and which need frequent updating; software can really take the load off a project which is fast moving and where you need to keep track;
- need a number of resources – e.g. more than five – **especially** when those resources are shared with other projects;
- are expensive; if your project budget is over what your organization considers is an appropriate authority level for you then you will benefit from the additional monitoring support this software gives;

77

MAKING PROJECT MANAGEMENT WORK FOR YOU

> ➤ involve sponsors who require regular reports. A computer generated GANTT chart, with milestones and progress bars impresses a project board much more than a hand-drawn effort, **even if** you use different coloured pencils!

and when **you**

> ➤ understand project management techniques well enough to understand what it is telling you and
> ➤ are comfortable using IT so that you drive the software not the other way around.

Remember, you can use other software to control simple projects. A word processor will allow you to list tasks, and to do simple scheduling. A spreadsheet will produce charts (including GANTT charts) and graphics, and a database can hold and sort a wide variety of data.

You can find out what software is available by looking at the *Software Users Yearbook,* or online in the *Datapro Software Directory* and other similar files. The PC magazines carry reviews of new software, which will help you to find a product that suits you. Some of the main packages are listed at Appendix B, but remember that new products are coming out all the time.

And finally . . .

A project management approach can help you to structure your work and achieve more. In this final chapter we have looked at:

- ➤ how to use these techniques in your everyday job
- ➤ things to look out for in running multiple projects
- ➤ when to use project management software and
- ➤ how to get the best out of it.

It's up to you now. Further reading is at Appendix 1. Good luck with your projects!

Appendix 1
Further reading

Chapter 1 What is project management?

Andersen, E. S., *Goal directed project management*, London, Kogan Page in association with Coopers & Lybrand, 1987.

Black, K., *Project management for library and information service professionals*. (Aslib Know How Guide), London, Aslib, 1996.
  Kirsten Black is Systems Manager at de Montfort University Library. Mainly IT projects.

Lock, D., *Project management*, 5th edn, Aldershot, Gower, 1994.
  Used by the Open University, and probably the standard book for anyone interested in project management. Comprehensive, with a bias towards construction and engineering projects.

O'Connell, F., *How to run successful projects: guide to structured project management* (Prentice-Hall BCS Practitioner Series), Englewood Cliffs, NJ, Prentice-Hall, 1993.
  This guide from the British Computer Society is good for IT-based projects.

Turner, R., *Handbook of project based management: improving the process for achieving strategic objectives* (Henley Management Series), Maidenhead, McGraw, 1993.

Chapter 2 Defining the project

British Standards Institute, *Guide to project management*, BS: 6079, London, BSI, 1996.

Chapter 3 Project organization

Central Computer and Telecommunications Agency, *PRINCE pocket book*, London, HMSO, 1994.

79

Central Computer and Telecommunications Agency, *PRINCE in small projects*, London, HMSO, 1994.

Both these short guides from CCTA give a good layman's introduction to the PRINCE methodology.

Chapter 4   Planning the project

Haynes, M. E., *Project management: from idea to implementation* (Kogan Page Better Management Skills), London, Kogan Page, 1990.

This short (78 page) book is particularly good on defining and planning the project.

Chapter 5   Project management techniques

Central Computer and Telecommunications Agency, *Management of project risk* (Management of risk library), London, HMSO, 1994.

Central Computer and Telecommunications Agency, *An introduction to managing project risk* (Management of risk library), London, HMSO, 1995.

Both these texts from CCTA are clearly written and explain the concept of risk in simple terms, with more detail on the risk checklist approach and how to use it.

Reiss, G., *Project management demystified: today's tools and techniques*. 2nd edn, London, Chapman and Hall, 1995.

If my book has whetted your appetite to know more this is the book to read next. Particularly good on network analysis, PERT and critical path.

Chapter 6   Implementing the project

Burton, C. and Michael, N., *A practical guide to project management: how to make it work in your organisation*, London, Kogan Page, 1992.

Randolph, W. A. and Posner, B. Z., *Getting the job done: managing project teams and task forces for success*, Englewood Cliffs, NJ, Prentice-Hall, 1995.

This quirky book ('the One Minute Manager's book for planning and managing projects') has good points on motivation and resolving conflicts.

Chapter 7 What to do when things go wrong

Morris, W. G. and Hough, G. H., *The anatomy of major projects: a study of reality in project management*, London, Wiley, 1987.

Willcocks, L. and Griffiths, C., *Are major IT projects worth the risk?* Oxford, Oxford Institute of Information Management, 1994.

Chapter 8 Evaluation

Central Computer and Telecommunications Agency, *PRINCE project evaluation*, London, HMSO, 1994.

Chapter 9 The real world

Turner, R., *Project manager as change agent*, Maidenhead, McGraw, 1996.

Lowery, G., *Managing projects with Microsoft Project*, New York, Van Nostrand Reinhold, 1992.

Clear explanations of how to use one of the market leaders in project management software.

Appendix 2
Project management software

There are well over a hundred different packages sold specifically as project management software, as well as all the spreadsheets, word processors and databases which can provide some of the facilities.

The following lists just a few of the best known, but this is an area of very rapid change. Check with databases such as *Datapro software directory* or *Softbase reviews* or the hardcopy *Software user's yearbook* for what is currently available. Most PC magazines carry reviews of the latest releases of micro-based software to keep you up to date.

All the software listed below is mid-price, runs on micros and is reasonably available. It will produce charts (GANTT, PERT, resource) and support scheduling and resource allocation. Most will also allow resource levelling (where the software delays tasks until you have enough resource to complete them) – useful if you know what you are doing.

As with other software, if you are considering buying any project management software try to find out more about it **before** you buy. Contact the vendor or, better still, the user group – the Web is a good place to start – and ask to see it in operation on some live sites so you can decide if it meets your needs.

Prices indicated below are for single users and exclude VAT. Shop around, you may be able to do better. Network prices depend on number of users etc.

£ = under £500
££ = £500 – £1000
£££ = £1000 – £1500

APPENDIX 2: PROJECT MANAGEMENT SOFTWARE

SuperProject 4.0

Publisher: Computer Associates
Runs on: All IBM PCs – DOS, Windows, OS/2.
Price: ££
Well-established package with over 100,000 users world-wide.

Micro Planner Manager 1.3

Publisher: Micro Planning International
Runs on: Apple
Price: ££
The Apple product from a publisher with a stable of PM software for most platforms and pockets. About 7000 users world-wide. Has features for beginners and professionals.

Project 4.0

Publisher: Microsoft
Runs on: All IBM PCs, Apple; Windows
Price: £
One of the most popular programs on the market. Huge user base. Has Microsoft helpful tools (tips, wizards) and interfaces with Excel and Word. Does the usual things, and latest version is easier to use than previous.

Project Manager Workbench (PMW) 3.02

Publisher: ABT
Runs on: IBM, laptops and networks
Price: £££
Heavyweight professional tool. Over 120,000 users world-wide. Particularly strong report writer.

Index

acceptance, project 59
accommodation 14, 37, 58
achievements 55
activities 22, 43, 54
actuals 45
adjusting 5–6, 63–6
approval 5, 13–16
arrow diagram 43
assumptions 12–13, 61
authority, limit of 50
authorizing body 14–16, 18, 19
availability 36–7

BAC *see* Business Assurance Coordinator
benefits 2, 5, 9, 15–16, 70
blame, negative effects of 64
brainstorming 8
British Standards Institute 79
budget 22, 55, 63–5, 69, 72
budget profiling 44–7, 63
bulletin boards 24
business acceptance letter 59
Business Assurance Coordinator 21
business case 5, 14, 15, 18, 19
business impact 49

CBA *see* cost benefit analysis
CCTA *see* Central Computer and Telecommunications Agency
Central Computer and Telecommunications Agency 50, 80
Chair 19
change 57–8
change requests 58
charts
    bar 41, 42
    budget control 47, 54
    flow 42
    GANTT 34, 39–42, 54, 61, 76, 77

PERT 42–3, 76
checkpoint reports 23, 56
checkpoints 35
colleagues 8
commitments 66, 69
communication 5, 22, 24, 57, 62, 71, 75
compatibility 12
completion 58–9
confirmation, written 37
constraints 2, 5, 11–12, 34
consultants 45
consumables 45
contingency 16, 64, 69
contracts 45, 66
cost-benefit analysis 16, 69
costing 44–5, 72
costs 2, 9, 15
CPA 43
CPM *see* critical path method
CPS *see* critical path scheduling
critical path 5, 42
critical path analysis 43
critical path method 42
critical path scheduling 43
critical success factors 11, 27–8, 63, 70
CSFs *see* critical success factors
customers 8

danger signals 61
dates, start and end 34, 35, 41
dead time 64
deadlines 34, 35, 62
definition, project 4–5, 7–17
deliverables 15, 37–8, 56–7, 70
disasters, how to avoid 60
dispute resolution, 75
documentation, 58
doing the job *see* implementation
duration, 31–3, 34, 41, 44, 61, 71

INDEX

elapsed time 33
environment 72–3
equipment 14, 37, 58
evaluation, 6, 68–73
events 43
exception reports 66–7
expectations 8, 12
expenses 44, 45

failure 67
feasiblity 9
fitness for purpose 63
fixed price 45
flexibility 41, 62, 65, 76
follow-up review 70

GANTT charts *see* charts
guesstimates 13

highlight reports 22, 56

implementation, 5, 38, 53–9, 60
implementation, phased 65
investment appraisal 16
issues 22, 55

lag 33
lead time 33, 37
legal requirements 11
line managers 8

meetings
    checkpoint 55
    project board 23
    team 23, 55
Micro Planner Manager 1.3 83
Microsoft Project 4.0 77, 83
milestones 31, 34, 37, 41, 75
monitoring 5, 54–7, 60, 61
motivatation 58
multiple projects 75–8
Murphy's laws 60

network analysis 43–4
newsletters 23

non-activities 43

objectives 2–3, 7–9, 27, 37, 62–3, 65, 70, 75
opportunities 2, 5
opportunity cost 15
options 57, 61, 64
organization, project 18–24
organizational culture 49
outcomes 27
out-of-scope 9
outputs 15, 37–8, 70
overspend 63, 76

PAT *see* project assurance team
pay-back period 15, 16
perfectionism, distorting effect of 63
PERT 32
PERT charts *see* charts
plan, initial 14–15
planning 5, 25–38
plans, good 25–7
post-project review 68
PRINCE 12, 18, 20, 38, 59, 81
priorities 48, 52, 75
problems 22, 47, 57
    business impact of 61
    how to resolve 63–6
    how to spot 61–3
products 14, 37–8
progress 62, 75
progress monitoring 41
project assurance team 56
project board 18, 22, 46, 56, 66
Project Evaluation and Review
    Technique *see* PERT
project manager 18, 21, 48
Project Manager Workbench (PMW) 3.02 83
project review 59
projects, how to recognize 2

quality 27, 37, 38, 54, 55, 65, 70
    poor 62–3
quality criteria 63

85

quality plan 27, 56, 70
quality review 50, 56

realism, importance of 13, 71
replanning 64
reporting methods 22–4
reports, final 57
resource allocation 35–7, 71, 75
resource calendars 76
resource pool 75, 76
resources 2, 5, 71, 75, 77
    changing 65–6
    human 14, 35
    other 14–15, 37
    over-allocation 76
    shared 76
responsibility 64
risk 2, 5, 13, 47, 75, 80
    how to calculate 50
    score 51
risk analysis 5, 47, 61
risk checklist 47, 50
risk factors 47–50

scheduling 31–5, 71, 75
scope 4, 9–11
scope, changing 65
Senior Finance 20–1
Senior Technical 20
Senior User 19–20
sequencing 43
skills 5, 14, 35, 72
slack 33, 44
slippage 34, 49, 61–2
software 76–8, 82–3
specification 27, 62
spend 46, 63
stages 4–6, 26, 30, 75
standards 11, 27, 38, 50
stopping the project 66
success factors *see* critical success factors
success, how to measure 69–70

SuperProject 4.0 83
suppliers 49, 58, 61, 66

TAC *see* Technical Assurance
    Coordinator
task allocation 36
task analysis 28–9
tasks 14, 26
    activity based 32
    critical 28, 42
    dependent 30, 33, 71
    next 55
    non-critical 42, 62
    overlapping 30, 33
    parallel 30, 33, 42
    related 30
    relationships 30–1, 34, 41
    unit based 31
team 72, 75
Technical Assurance Coordinator 20
techniques 39–52
time and materials 45
time management 28
timescales 2, 26, 41, 55, 63, 69, 77
    changing 64–5
    slipping 61–2
tolerance 16, 64
track record supplier 49

UAC *see* User Assurance Coordinator
uncertainty 13
underspend 63
User Assurance Coordinator 20

value added tax 16, 45
VAT *See* value added tax
vision 9

Web pages 24
windows of opportunity 34, 62
working practices 12